"This is an inspiring must-read for every leader in the post-pandemic economy! *Competing in the New World of Work* provides compelling, research-based methods for how to maximize collaboration and inclusion within your team, how to anticipate change and pivot toward new opportunities, and how to make your organization radically adaptable to a future that's coming at you faster than you think."

—JACK CANFIELD, founder, Transformational Leadership Council; coauthor, *The Success Principles*

"Every new era opens with its crystallizing crisis. World War II accelerated aviation by twenty years, sparking the jet age that transformed travel. The pandemic accelerated the transformation of work. Ferrazzi has written the bible on the fluid adaptability that organizations now need to survive and thrive."

—SCOTT COOK, cofounder, Intuit

"If you read one business book about leading your company in the post-pandemic world, this should be the one. *Competing in the New World of Work* elegantly coaches you on the leadership competency necessary to support a high-performance team in this new world. You'll learn how to collaborate, how to retain talent, how to see around corners, and how to thrive in an age of disruption. Don't go back to the old rules of work—read this book and go forward!"

—PETER H. DIAMANDIS, founder and Executive Chairman, XPRIZE and Singularity University; *New York Times* bestselling author, *Abundance*, *Bold*, and *The Future Is Faster Than You Think*

"*The New World of Work* is a fascinating examination of what it means to successfully adapt and compete in the post-pandemic era. Ferrazzi and his team have delivered a timely and powerful guide to help readers navigate and thrive in this unprecedented period of opportunity."

—TAMI ERWIN, CEO, Verizon Business

"The post-pandemic world will require a renewed take on teamwork, and *Competing in the New World of Work* should be required reading for leaders at all levels. From teaching you how to collaborate exponentially to managing your team's resilience in an era of constant stress, Ferrazzi's latest book provides compelling, research-based methods for how to upskill your team leadership competency throughout the organization."

—JIM FITTERLING, Chairman and CEO, Dow

"In a turbulent world, you have three options. You can resist change and become obsolete, react to change and struggle to survive, or anticipate change and adapt in advance. This is a hands-on guide for choosing the third path."

—ADAM GRANT, #1 *New York Times* bestselling author, *Think Again*; host, TED podcast *WorkLife with Adam Grant*

"Unsurprisingly, Ferrazzi has done it again! His new book, *Competing in the New World of Work*, so beautifully describes—and teaches you how to develop—the leadership competencies necessary to help you and your team 'radically adapt' for this new post-pandemic, hybrid world. The future of work is now, and this is a must-read for every leader and entrepreneur."

—MINDY GROSSMAN, President and CEO, WW International

"A new world and new way of working are here. Ferrazzi, Gohar, and Weyrich deliver an excellent blueprint for success that we, as leaders across industries, will find beneficial as we continue to manage change in an ever-evolving, agile world."

—CECE MORKEN, CEO, Headspace Inc.

"Winning today means being prepared for tomorrow. Only highly adaptive organizations that embrace new models and make the critical connection points between people, products, and processes are positioned to lead the future. Ferrazzi's articulation of what it takes to prepare for this exciting future is equal parts prophetic and practical."

—DIRK VAN DE PUT, Chairman and CEO, Mondelēz International

COMPETING
IN THE
NEW
WORLD
OF WORK

HOW RADICAL ADAPTABILITY
SEPARATES THE BEST FROM THE REST

COMPETING IN THE *NEW* WORLD OF WORK

KEITH FERRAZZI
KIAN GOHAR, AND NOEL WEYRICH

HARVARD BUSINESS REVIEW PRESS

BOSTON, MASSACHUSETTS

Library of Congress Cataloging-in-Publication Data

Names: Ferrazzi, Keith, author. | Gohar, Kian, author. | Weyrich, Noel,
    author.
Title: Competing in the new world of work : how radical adaptability
    separates the best from the rest / by Keith Ferrazzi, Kian Gohar, and
    Noel Weyrich.
Description: Boston, MA : Harvard Business Review Press, [2021] | Includes
    index.
Identifiers: LCCN 2021034686 (print) | LCCN 2021034687 (ebook) |
    ISBN 9781647821951 (hardcover) | ISBN 9781647821968 (ebook)
Subjects: LCSH: Organizational change. | Organizational effectiveness. |
    COVID-19 Pandemic, 2020—Economic aspects. | Industrial management. |
    Success in business. | Organizational behavior.
Classification: LCC HD58.8 .F47 2021 (print) | LCC HD58.8 (ebook) |
    DDC 658.4/06—dc23
LC record available at https://lccn.loc.gov/2021034686
LC ebook record available at https://lccn.loc.gov/2021034687

ISBN: 978-1-64782-195-1
eISBN: 978-1-64782-196-8

The paper used in this publication meets the requirements of the American National Standard for Permanence of Paper for Publications and Documents in Libraries and Archives Z39.48-1992.

*To the endlessly radically adaptable team at Ferrazzi Greenlight.
In the years to come, may we continue to co-elevate
and transform the teams who transform the world.*

Contents

COMPETING
IN THE
NEW
WORLD
OF WORK

Radical Adaptability

Black Rock Desert in northern Nevada is probably the worst place on earth for thousands of people to gather during the last week of August. Midday temperatures on the lifeless salt flats hover near 110°F. The nearest electrical connections and running water taps are almost ten miles away. You need goggles and a face mask for protection from the sudden dust storms with their fifty-mile-per-hour winds. And yet, since 1991, Black Rock Desert has drawn as many as eighty thousand people annually to the Burning Man celebration.

By design, Burning Man is a strange and otherworldly place, where many of the outside world's rules don't apply. For nine days out of the year, a community springs up in Black Rock Desert as a social experiment in which money is forbidden and extreme creativity is celebrated. It's the only place you'll ever see Deadheads and classical musicians composing new harmonies together, while anarchic pyromaniacs join with tech elites to build gigantic flaming artworks, new age spiritualists exchange deep thoughts with business executives, and tree huggers work side-by-side with gun lovers to maintain the campgrounds and protect the fragile desert ecosystem.

It all works, not in spite of the harsh desert environment but because of it. The shared communal predicament of enduring such adverse conditions sustains a deep sense of commitment to a shared mission and belonging amid scorching heat, frigid nights, and whirling dust storms. "Communities are not produced by sentiment or mere good-will," Burning Man cofounder Larry Harvey once said. "They grow out of a shared struggle."[1] The struggle for existence is what drives collaboration at Burning Man. The unforgiving desert is a crucible for creativity.

Keith Ferrazzi had been going to Burning Man every year for sixteen years when the pandemic shut down plans for the 2020 gathering. At the time, he reflected with coauthor Kian Gohar, who is also a "burner," on the parallels between the world's shared struggles and the lessons offered by the world of Burning Man. The founders of Burning Man refer to it as an "experiment in temporary community dedicated to radical self-expression and radical self-reliance."[2] After many months of research, some of our team members who had been to "the Burn" realized that this depiction also precisely describes the pandemic. Burning Man is a small and deliberate social experiment, and the pandemic turned out to be its own kind of social experiment for the workplace, an accidental and tragic experiment, conducted on a global scale.

Without doubt, the pandemic foisted on the globe tragic levels of adversity and an unwelcome social experiment in grief and privation. And yet, because of the hardships it placed on our lives and how it required us to react, the pandemic also turned out to be a source of tremendous insight, creativity, innovation, and community for many of us, similar to the shared experience of thriving in the desert. We hope it will be a powerful and positive inflection point for us all, and we aspire to share the most important leadership lessons learned through this book.

Adaptation happens to be the *one thing* that human beings do better than any other animal on the planet. We're not the biggest, we're not the fastest, and we don't have the sharpest teeth or the strongest claws, yet we are the dominant species on earth, thanks to our extreme and relentless adaptability to change.

Work Isn't Working

For decades, Keith and Kian have preached that industry disruption has been so painful precisely because leaders have *failed* to adapt their strategies and ways of working to the unique demands of rapidly accelerating disruption. The two of us have designed and facilitated hundreds of leadership team engagements globally, coaching executives to harness innovation and exponential technologies to build a better future. In our experience, it's always a challenge to persuade these executives that their team cultures are stuck in the past and desperately inadequate for the future ahead. The competencies required for team leadership have been shifting for decades, and it's time to recognize the advantages of meeting these trends. How we work hasn't been working for a long time, but we've continued to cling to outdated ways of work as though we were hanging by our fingernails over an abyss.

Then, in 2020, the entire world was struck with a level of disruption that few had ever imagined. The need for a new level of adaptability in the workplace became a dire necessity, not just a competency of the truly best. All the practices Keith and Kian had been recommending to executive teams for years suddenly became must-do items rather than nice-to-haves. In a single year, adversity ushered in more changes in ways of doing business than we had seen in decades. It was a weird new world of work, a great laboratory in so many ways, one that offered all of us a blank slate on which we could reinvent how we work, how we experiment at work, and who we invite into our conversations.

From our perspective, a window of opportunity had flown wide open, and we were excited to hear many people acknowledge how the crisis had brought out the best in them and their teams. "We know how to do this," said Cathy Clegg, leader of transformation initiatives at GM manufacturing. "This is where GM truly shines." She and others, when forced to improvise, rose to the challenge with unprecedented levels of tenacity, innovation, and some of the so-called soft skills of leadership: humility and vulnerability. We had been granted permission to explore without borders, the way we had felt free to ride bicycles at midnight across the roadless flat desert floor at Burning Man.

When leaders were compelled to set aside red tape and delegate more decision-making, results flowed faster than ever before. Companies responded by collaborating more intensively and communicating more thoroughly. Team members were more candid with each other and spoke more freely and directly because the emergency eliminated opportunities for conflict avoidance and passive-aggressive communication. Team members also became more generous. They broke out of siloed that's-not-my-job behaviors. And out of sincere concern for each other, they asked, "How can I help?" The crisis set teams free to take action. And it made teams better.

All around the world, big companies and small businesses alike were forced to discover new processes, new markets, and new business models that proved to be lasting sources of competitive advantage. London's top Michelin-star restaurants got into the business of home deliveries and cook-it-yourself meal kits.[3] Stagekings, an Australian theater set-building company, pivoted to making home office desks under the brand name IsoKing—and looked to expand to Europe.[4] Spice seller Diaspora Co., with its suppliers in India locked down, switched to taking preorders as a cash-flow strategy and saw sales surge 35 percent.[5] In Taiwan, where airlines devoid of passengers in early 2020 put a new emphasis on shipping packages, China Airlines enjoyed a surprisingly profitable second quarter.[6] Even in a radically disrupted business environment, companies learned they could thrive if they could crack the code of radical adaptability and master its lessons.

At the same time, though, working in a crisis left many feeling stressed and worn down. The hours were long, and all the improvised jury-rigged systems and processes suffered from frequent breakdowns. Without proper support for sustaining these new modes of work, many companies were merely "crisis adapting." Without the right tools and coaching, some felt overwhelmed and defeated. Many people had a hard time seeing the magic and the possibility. They wanted it all to stop. They just wanted to go back to work.

That notion gripped Keith with a sense of urgency bordering on panic. What if this new world of work ended up permanently tarred by its association with the pandemic? What if tradition and inertia proved to be so strong that all the bad old habits snapped back into effect as soon as the pandemic ended? Crises are so exhausting that it's natural to want to return to the comfort of the familiar. But if we were to do that and resume working the way we had before, such a return would be yet another disaster, one that would last long after the pandemic had passed into history.

At Ferrazzi Greenlight, where our job is to accelerate team transformation, we'd noticed that some teams we were coaching had adapted extremely well in certain areas, while other teams had proven innovative in very different ones. Keith began organically piecing together a methodology for clients composed of insights and best practices gleaned from the others. He began hosting small virtual gatherings of clients to exchange ideas. That's when he realized what was needed was a central forum for exploring and sharing what the best of the best were doing to survive.

It became clear to us at Ferrazzi Greenlight that we should never go back to the way things were. We couldn't afford to lose such hard-won momentum. So we pledged to turn the experiences and lessons learned during the crisis into big wins for our customers, for our companies, and for each other. We would preserve all the practices we had honed during the crisis. And while we're at it, we pledged to make our work in this new world more purposeful, more meaningful, and more humane.

Let's never just go back to work.

Let's go forward!

Research Basis for This Book

At Ferrazzi Greenlight's research institute, we launched what we thought at the time would be a several-month project called Go Forward to Work (GFTW). We recruited change agents from big companies, entrepreneurs, and some of the most well regarded thought leaders—people who shared our vision of how the rules of work were being rewritten day-by-day and didn't want the opportunity squandered. We wanted to create a place to stop and cocreate what the future would look like five years forward: a place to analyze how much change would be necessary and what exciting possibilities lay ahead, all in light of the best practices we were seeing and collectively sharing from our pandemic experiences.

To that end, we developed partnerships with Harvard Business Review Press, Dell Technologies, Salesforce, SAP, EY, Anaplan, LHH, WW, Headspace, World 50, and many other brands and associations. Our teams of researchers supported the production of dozens of stories appearing in *Forbes*, *Fast Company*, the *Wall Street Journal*, and *Harvard Business Review*. We reached thousands of leaders through team engagements, coaching sessions, and virtual town halls in partnership with our GFTW faculty fellows (practitioners and thought leaders who guided and published our research) and GFTW fellows (internal change agents from across industries and corporations). We leveraged online conferences and podcasts with direct calls to action to join this movement and contribute to our collective research at GoForwardToWork .com.

We knew we had a responsibility to not let this once-in-a-lifetime opportunity pass us by. And so we documented all the innovations and best practices that were happening on the fly and considered how they could lead our vision in the years to come. And we crowdsourced a research-based methodology for what leadership means in a radically volatile world.

A New World of Work Is Emerging

Before the pandemic, Keith and Kian had been to hundreds of events exploring the *future of work*, a term that in our view was just a loosey-goosey feel-good phrase for intellectual pontification by thought leaders and executives who thought the future of work was on some distant horizon. But both of us struggled with this term, because the so-called future of work had been unfolding in real time all around us for years before the pandemic. And although we were screaming from the rooftops about the need for executive teams to change, many companies just punted and operated in a manner reminiscent of yesteryear. But suddenly in 2020, this future of work became *the present of work*, and every leader realized they had to pay attention. They had to pivot or get left behind.

Our research at GFTW discovered commonalities among those who were thriving and revealed the difficulties that most leaders were struggling with. We found that the urgency of the situation melted the frozen routines and the ossified protocols that had long posed obstacles to growth and change. We came to see a new world of work emerging from the old world (see figure 1-1). In the new pandemic world, companies attempted things that they would never have tried to do under normal circumstances in the old world. Projects nobody wanted to take on suddenly made sense. Digital transformation projects that previously had a five-year implementation plan materialized literally overnight. Product development cycle times were reduced to fractions of their prior times. Small, accidental experiments bore fruit that led to greater successes. Companies rethought their workplace physical footprint and shuttered their office buildings. Like never before, they became open to flexible work arrangements and pivoted week by week, cocreating major strategic choices on the fly. The levels of mutual support were astounding as team members *co-elevated*—they lifted each other up in an esprit de corps of resourcefulness and experimentation.

FIGURE 1-1

The old and new worlds of work compared

When facing uncertainty	THE OLD WORLD OF WORK		THE NEW WORLD OF WORK	When facing uncertainty
Slower, less innovative	Authority		Co-elevation	More, better ideas
Limited by structures	Hierarchy		Agility	Pivots and sprints forward
Team overwhelmed	Personal resilience		Team resilience	Peer-to-peer support
Caught off guard	Reacts to change		Foresees change	Ready to act
Risk averse to change	Prioritizes core business		Seeks constant reinvention	Discards old assumptions
Limited flexibility	Talent management		Lego block workforce	Versatile and fluid
Doesn't inspire action	Mission focused		Purpose driven	Drives every desicison

Battles waves and trudges through to the finish line

Floats above turbulent waves and wins the race

"Covid became the common enemy," recounted Pam Klyn, vice president of product and brands at Whirlpool. When the pandemic forced the closure of the R&D labs at Whirlpool, workers resorted to testing washing machine parts in their home garages and basements. They exchanged parts to be tested by meeting fellow team members at arranged spots on specific stretches of interstate highways. Once Whirlpool's new technical center is ready to open in southwest Michigan, Klyn's teams have told her they want to take their work forward, not backward. "It's about sustaining energy," Klyn explained. "People want to hang on to the gains."

Radical Adaptability: A Blueprint for Success in the New World of Work

From our research interviewing more than two thousand leaders through the pandemic, we identified a consistent pattern of successful leadership competencies across industries and synthesized that into a new leadership methodology for a future of accelerating change and uncertainty. We call this methodology *radical adaptability* (figure 1-2). It presents all the lessons of crisis leadership in the form of a sustainable model for leading continuous change through the coming years of unexpected turmoil, opportunity, and transformation.

The seven chapters that follow represent best practices in how to build a radically adaptable future to compete in this new world of work. Chapters 2 through 5 describe how to build a radically adaptable *team*, and chapters 6 through 8 introduce how to leverage that team to build a radically adaptable *organization*. Together these seven chapters form an infinite loop that reinforces radical adaptability and transformation.

Chapters 2 through 5 tackle core leadership competencies that, when stacked on top of each other, create a circular flow state for teams to operate at peak performance:

FIGURE 1-2

Radical adaptability

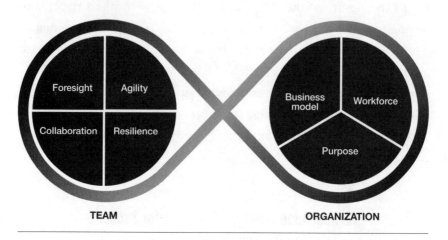

1. *Collaborate through inclusion.* Embrace the possibility of richer diversity of virtual, remote, and hybrid teamwork to drive innovation exponentially forward.

2. *Lead through enterprise agile.* Extend and expand the cultural ethos of short-term sprints that kept us on our trajectory during the crisis, and find an operating system that allows us to thrive sustainably amid continued volatility.

3. *Promote team resilience.* Bounce forward in the face of setbacks and recognize that good leaders strive to maintain the emotional and physical energies of the team.

4. *Develop active foresight.* Learn to see around corners to avoid unsuspected risk and to systematically explore new possibilities.

The final three chapters present an operating model for your radically adaptable team to build a radically adaptable organization by deploying the radical adaptable team skills of collaboration, agility, resilience, and foresight to three enterprise-wide applications:

5. *Future-proof your business model.* Develop an ongoing process of experimentation to create and realize your company's future vision of itself.

6. *Build a Lego block workforce.* Redesign your workforce to support a flexible, nimble, cost-effective, and creative future.

7. *Supercharge your purpose.* Build a movement for radical adaptability by discovering and communicating your organization's long-term purpose.

The essence of radical adaptability is that it is predictive, proactive, and progressive, very unlike the typical response to change, which is inherently reactive and conformist. By definition, adaptability is the ability to adjust to new conditions. Adaptability is a coping mechanism. *Radical adaptability is a transformational mechanism.* Radical adaptability prompts you to constantly anticipate change, reinterpret it, and transform yourself through change. Through radical adaptability, you embrace the new world of work and grow with it, while others merely adjust and adapt to it.

Competing in the New World of Work

We believe radical adaptability best describes what every company can and *must* do within the next eighteen months to leap forward five years. Otherwise, you'll be left behind in the dust by your competitors. In 2020, we accelerated change that was years in the planning, even though the pandemic was exhausting. Going forward, we believe you can thrive and win the future, *if* you use the research methodology offered by radical adaptability and do it in ways that strengthen your organization and not wear it out. The urgency of change is real. The challenge is how to maintain your energy and passion through change and not crumble from its strain and pace.

It has become clear to us that sustaining competitive advantage in a post-pandemic world will require leaders to master radical adaptability every day and in every role in the organization. The specifics are different for every company, but the radical-adaptability framework will inspire leaders to catapult their organizations forward, make up for lost time, embrace new realities, and win new frontiers.

Though the word *transformation* suffers from severe overuse these days, radical adaptability requires true transformative leadership. Traditional work processes, business models, and workforce structures will not prepare us for the future that's rising up faster than most would assume. For example, take a moment to visualize what you assume might be the reality of your job or industry in five years. There's a good chance that all those things need to get done in the next eighteen months if you want to be anything more than a follower and if you don't want to lose ground to your competitors. The hurdle for success has been raised exponentially, and the terrain has become simultaneously rockier. This new world of work requires a new set of attitudes, processes, and practices that will achieve not just 10 percent improvement over yesteryear, but $10X$ transformation to prepare you for a future that is faster than you think.

The difference is all in how we choose to go forward.

Embedded in our innate human gift for adaptability is our instinctive drive to create meaning out of the ashes of catastrophe. Disasters have always served humankind as engines for innovation and progress. The Great Chicago Fire of 1871 also gave Chicago the most advanced fire prevention laws on earth. Cholera epidemics in the 1800s gave New York City world-class health and sanitation codes. The deadly 1995 Kobe earthquake provided Japan with the world's strictest and smartest building regulations. In a similar way, the Covid-19 pandemic provided us with a new set of world-class codes for work, if we go forward with them.

Disasters don't just destroy. They reveal. They uncover the weaknesses in human structures—both physical and social—that had long outlived their usefulness when disaster struck. That was true in 1871, when wood-framed buildings in Chicago's tightly packed downtown burned like matchsticks. It was also true in 2020, when hierarchies and bureaucracies were exposed for their inadequacies while teams and networks of teams rose up and declared, "This is when we are at our best."

The pandemic revealed in ways big and small much of what hadn't been working with work for a long time: top-down, overplanned, draining, reactive, bureaucratic, static, and narrowly mission oriented. Now we've all been invited to join a new world of work that has been emerging for many years, one that's collaborative and inclusive, agile, resilient, anticipatory, reinventive, flexible, and purpose-driven.

New ways of thinking don't come easy. Sometimes it takes immersion in a new, strange world to recognize that the familiar world has not been serving you very well.

Leading in the New World of Work

Some years ago, Keith brought one of the world's top automotive executives to Burning Man, someone we'll call François, for confidentiality purposes. François showed up in a sport shirt, khaki shorts, and a state of mind that was curious but highly skeptical.

Once he got over the mild shock of what everyone else was wearing (or not wearing), François naturally gravitated toward the hundreds of gearheads who create Burning Man's mutant vehicles—bizarre mobile machines that are a mix of engineering genius and artistic inspiration. A 2019 *Motor Trend* feature on Burning Man included images of a fire-breathing dragon built on the chassis of a GMC Safari van. Another featured vehicle looked like a forty-foot steel shark with the guts of a Cadillac, and yet another was a double-decker bus expanded to a quad-decker and tricked out in LEDs.[7]

François spent a lot of time with the mutant vehicle creators. One in particular was an eccentric genius who, François discovered, was a design engineer at one of François' competitors, and who kept spewing fantastical musings of what was possible in the future of mobility and how hard he had to work to make this dream a reality. François assumed he knew the car industry very well, but this mad genius showed him how much he lacked in inspiration and imagination. François was shaken to his core.

One night, he brought that eccentric genius engineer back to the camp for something Keith calls the *otherness exercise*. Keith asks each guest to return at dinner time with a stranger they have strong judgments about—someone who, outside the world of Burning Man, they would consider strange and outrageous and would avoid. Over our meal, Keith facilitated the conversation as he would in a team-building exercise, prompting the dinner guests to get to know the stranger who they might have considered "the other," as a way to develop empathy and under-standing for the unknown. In business and in life, empathy is a certain path to expanding your insights and sense of possibility.

Before the end of Burning Man, François confided that his experi-ence left him questioning everything about his leadership style. He pon-dered why he hadn't offered his most creative people the chance to fully express themselves through their work, much as the wild genius engineer had. And he wondered if the excitement and engagement he had witnessed among the mutant vehicle makers could also be unleashed in his own team back at work. He'd begun to question whether he had unwittingly served as a tool of a hierarchy and a bureaucracy that no longer served him, his employees, or the company? By the end of the week, François had swapped out his sport shirt and khakis for a Day-Glo loincloth.

After Burning Man, François reentered his familiar world feeling newly energized and eager to pass the inspiration on to his team. He decided to create ways to listen to their ideas more carefully—both for-mally and informally—and to give them more freedom to make deci-sions at deeper levels of the company and to trust them to cocreate bolder solutions, with fewer intermittent checks and balances. The auto industry's transformation to electric power was then just on the rise, and although an enterprise commitment to transformation was far from articulated, some members of François's team insisted on working on what that transformation strategy could and should be. Over the next eighteen months, they developed some truly brilliant new designs and led the company to accelerated product development results that would not have happened otherwise.

The many months we spent in the strangeness of a pandemic exposed all of us to the same possibility of personal transformation that François faced at Burning Man. We could either duck into a tent and wait for the dust storm to pass or find our way to new heights by exploring the unknown through radical adaptability. During the pandemic, we witnessed how fast and how far people can go when they're given the chance to rise to the occasion and manage their way out of one crisis after another. That is the ethos of radical adaptability.

Shaping the Future

Building a new world of work won't be easy. The coming years of recovery and renewal offer a historic opportunity to remake our organizations and our futures, but only if we accept this as an inflection point for true reinvention. The radically adaptable way of leading described in this book is designed to future-proof both your personal leadership style and your business. That's because it is built on the assumption that for the foreseeable future, we will all be going forward to work in a new world of constant change and disruption. That's the promise of this book: to help you develop a sustainable leadership style and strategy to guide you through low tide, tsunamis, and fair seas. We firmly believe that the number one lesson from the pandemic must be that we have to develop a strategy to survive similar shocks in the future, be they events or the relentless disruption of technological and social change.

As this book goes to print, our GFTW research continues, and we extend to you our invitation to join the movement and contribute to the research, at GoForwardToWork.com. The coming pages represent the best practices and insights derived from more than a year of this crowdsourced research. To execute radical adaptability, however, the methodologies by themselves will not be enough to compete in a new world of work.

Why? Remember the name Tilly Smith.

In late 2004, Tilly Smith was a ten-year-old girl from Surrey, England, who was vacationing with her parents during winter break at a small, secluded oceanfront resort in Phuket, Thailand.

Tilly was strolling the beach with her mother when the water at their feet started behaving very strangely. "The sea was all frothy like on the top of a beer. It was bubbling," she would later recall.[8]

In school two weeks earlier, right before the winter break, Tilly had seen a documentary about the devastating Hawaiian tsunami of 1946, which killed ninety-six people in the seaside town of Hilo.[9] The video described how the tsunami had taken the people of Hilo by surprise because they had failed to recognize the danger signs when the waters in Hilo Bay began frothing and fizzing minutes before the big wave arrived.

Frightened by what she knew about the water bubbling at her feet, Tilly pulled on her mother's arm and warned her that a tsunami was on its way. Her mother was skeptical, but Tilly started screaming about her lesson in school. Tilly's mother finally relented, and she and Tilly's father spread the word. Hotel security cleared the beach, and the great Indian Ocean tsunami struck minutes later. In the hours that followed, more than two hundred thousand people were killed by tsunami waves all across the Indian Ocean basin. Thailand's coastal towns suffered tens of thousands of deaths, but the secluded beach where Tilly and her family were staying was the only beach in Thailand with zero fatalities.[10]

When Tilly returned home to England, she was hailed as a hero for saving more than a hundred lives that day, all because she'd learned her school lessons so well.[11] But that's not really what made her a hero.

It was important, of course, that Tilly had knowledge and insight about tsunamis and why the water was behaving so strangely. But that was only half the equation. What made Tilly a hero was her resolve, her belief in what she knew, and the courage it took to put her knowledge and insights into action.

Tilly knew something important about the world that her mother didn't. When Tilly's mother first tried to shrug off her daughter's warnings, Tilly didn't back down.

Instead, she got angry. She told her mother, "Right, I'm leaving you, because there is definitely going to be a tsunami." That was enough to impress Tilly's mother that her daughter might be right. Together with Tilly's father, they alerted hotel security. Minutes later, when the tsunami struck, all the guests and staff were safely sheltered in the upper floors of the resort hotel.[12]

Courage, not knowledge, is what made Tilly Smith a hero. Her knowledge was essential, but without the courage of her convictions—without expressing her righteous anger to her mother in that crucial moment—her knowledge about tsunamis would have died with her that day, along with her parents and everyone else on the beach.

From all the committed change agents who contributed to this book, this is their challenge to you: to be this kind of hero. To be like Tilly. Be the lonely voice who speaks up because you can see what's coming in the new world of work. Take this knowledge, absorb these insights, and then exercise the courage required to be the radically adaptable leader who puts them into action. And when your colleagues push back, when maybe even your boss tells you that you can't pull this off, that it won't work—don't back down.

Think of Tilly Smith.

Stand by what you know to be true.

Fight for the actions you know are needed to compete as a radically adaptable leader, and win in this new world of work.

Show you have courage that's at least the equal of the world's most heroic ten-year-old.

Collaborate through Inclusion

The pandemic forced a sudden revolution in collaboration at most organizations. The necessity to begin operating through remote work exposed a rising awareness of what has always been true: collaboration has nothing to do with *where* employees show up for work; it has everything to do with *how* they show up. Outcomes have always mattered more than presentee-ism, even if performance hasn't always been measured or rewarded that way.

As companies began reconsidering their policies toward remote work, there was a great deal of wrongheadedness in the debate. Many leaders continued to insist that physically proximate work is inherently the best form of collaboration, citing examples of teams that had lost productivity by doing remote work poorly. The trouble is that so many made the move to remote on a strict survival basis that they neglected to take full advantage of the opportunities remote work afforded. Relatively few organizations achieved higher levels of productivity by truly optimizing their remote work practices for greater collaboration and much wider inclusion.

At the same time, 2020 sparked a new awakening to the importance of diversity, equality, and inclusion in the workplace, as companies made earnest commitments to diversity metrics in areas such as pay equality, positional equality, and board equality. Through discussions with thousands of executives at the Go Forward to Work (GFTW) Institute, it became clear that leaders need to think beyond these metrics and strive to create an authentic culture of inclusion and belonging. There needs to be a matching commitment to having diverse voices heard within organizations.

Telva McGruder, chief diversity, equity and inclusion (DEI) officer at General Motors, said it well: "If we can leverage the call for inclusion today around eradicating racism—using this as the hook to really get leaders to open up to let people be heard—it's the right step forward for unleashing innovation overall."

At Ferrazzi Greenlight, our coaching has long emphasized the important role of inclusion in collaboration, and the new world of work allows and requires that inclusion be accomplished at scale. Inclusion in the workplace must extend to race, ethnicity, gender, age, sexual orientation, and physical ability because it's the right thing to do and because all successful innovation and transformation benefits from including the full diversity of voices and perspectives.

The trouble, however, is that few corporate teams display the inclusive culture necessary to lead our diverse workforce through the challenges of business transformation. In fact, most teams lack the essential collaborative behaviors proven to be most effective among top-performing teams. For example, studies at the Ferrazzi Greenlight Research Institute (home of GFTW) have shown the following statistics:

- Only two in five executive teams begin the coaching program feeling that their teams are bound by caring, trusting, supportive relationships.

High-Return Practices for Competing in the New World of Work

1. Practice cocreation through co-elevation.
2. Break through silos by teaming out.
3. Hybridize teamwork for inclusion and crowdsourcing.
4. Deepen external partnerships.
5. Expand your personal coaches in a remote world.

- Some 74 percent of team members are conflict avoidant and lack the courage to speak their minds.

- Around 72 percent of team members do not believe that they and their peers collaborate on the most important business problems.

- Some 71 percent of team members report back-channel conversations and gossip that obstruct honest airings of issues, deflate morale, and prevent teams from coming together as a single unit.

Inclusion is the vital ingredient missing from these teams. As Telva put it, "Inclusion is not just in service of the DEI [diversity, equity and inclusion] agenda. It's core to any organization's capability to transform."

The pandemic forced many teams into crisis mode, and human nature bound them closer together in their unfamiliar, resource-deprived environment. Call it the Burning Man effect. Participants in GFTW research shared stories of becoming innovative out of urgency. They ignored turf to just get the job done, crowdsourced ideas, shut down silos, and brought their customers closer to them because the teams could no longer travel to the customers. They told of creating deeper partnerships with vendors because they had a stake in their vendors' survival.

Instead of grinding down vendors on price, the team members were calling to ask, "Are you OK?"

And in the most intimate form of collaboration, all of us were more readily open to each other as coaches for informal learning and professional development. We started realizing that there are people whose advice we could seek everywhere, but we had to reach out to them deliberately instead of waiting for the occasional serendipitous get-together.

From our perspective at Ferrazzi Greenlight, where we have been coaching teams toward collaboration and inclusion for twenty years, the pandemic revealed the efficacy of many practices we had long been advocating for. Back in September 2012, Keith hosted a webinar for *Harvard Business Review* called "How Virtual Teams Can Outperform Traditional Teams." Between 2012 and 2014, he wrote more than a dozen pieces for HBR on high-return practices for virtual and hybrid team effectiveness, all based on millions of dollars' worth of original research done by Ferrazzi Greenlight and its corporate partners.[1]

During the pandemic year of 2020 and afterward, we studied dozens of companies that had been suddenly immersed into the new world of virtual and remote work. When we introduced our high-return practices to these teams and then compared performance results to their pre-pandemic benchmarks, we documented sizable shifts in team efficacy across all the markers of high-performing teams. These markers included candor, accountability, and development. We also studied virtual teams that were not using our high-return practices and found that their performance had dropped. Virtual and remote teamwork *works*, but only if you do it right.

These and other discoveries about best practices and methodologies makes this the foundational chapter for radical adaptability. The chapter is organized in five steps that begin with your core team and show how to shift from traditional leadership competencies to co-elevating team competencies. From there we redefine and expand the definition of teams altogether. We show how to *team out* beyond internal silos and org chart boundaries. From there we move to using virtual tools to crowdsource solutions throughout the organization; we look at part-nering with vendors and clients and co-elevating with peers inside and outside the organization for growth and development. These fundamen-tal high-return practices for collaboration will be revisited throughout the book, and some of them are applicable in almost every chapter that follows.

Out of the pandemic, this new world of work has emerged with a dire need for new work rules in virtual, remote, asynchronous, and hybrid working styles. The pandemic introduced a culture of collabo-ration and inclusion that so many of us have advocated for so many years. Now we have a unique opportunity to institute permanent change.

"The money saved in rent and travel costs doesn't belong to the bot-tom line," said Martin Lindstrom, author of the bestseller *Buyology* and one of the world's top 20 business thinkers, according to Thinkers50. "It belongs instead to investments in collaborative culture. Now is the time to reinvent what organizational culture means."

Practice Cocreation through Co-elevation

In 2020, the pandemic forced companies into a new standard of highly collaborative behaviors that we saw over and over again in our research on high-performing co-elevating teams. For a long time, polite, coop-erative teamwork was sufficient to get the job done. Team members would operate independently, fulfilling their roles and assigned obliga-tions, and would only slip into actual collaboration when it was neces-sary. On high-performing teams, however, the objective is to go beyond cooperation and create a dynamic of constant and unbounded cocre-ation. On such teams, interdependent members share accountability for each other's results, pick each other up when one of them needs help, and share responsibility for crossing the finish line together. That's the essence of what we call *co-elevating teamwork*, when team members together create results that also raise their capabilities as individuals. The new tools for virtual and blended teamwork make this message more compelling and more suited for the new world of work, where teamwork moves beyond mere cooperation and becomes truly cocreative.

How Fox Factory became a co-elevating team

Mike Dennison was a relatively new CEO at Fox Factory in Northern California when 2020 presented him with a set of complex challenges: How do we take on the organizational reengineering demanded by the pandemic, in the backdrop of local wildfires, social unrest, customer lockdowns, and overstretched supply chains? And how do we do all this and still remain on course with our audacious strategy, to double the size of our business to $2 billion within five years?

Fox Factory designs and manufactures high-performance parts for snowmobiles, mountain bikes, motorcycles, all-terrain vehicles, off-road cars, trucks, and sport utility vehicles. The company traditionally operated as a set of product lines, with each product line leader accountable for its results. Mike was determined to bring the two divisions closer together, partly prompted by pandemic-related operational problems but mainly because cross-team collaboration toward unified goals would stimulate growth and create new value from team interdependency. Collaboration and inclusion—moving toward becoming a co-elevating team—was the way forward. In a virtual meeting with his newly integrated team members from around the country, Mike put the question on the table: "What can we do to increase our growth by 30 percent above and beyond acquisitions and the traditional growth plan?" He knew that Fox Factory's ambitious future growth would only be achieved through a total reengineering of the company's go-to-market and product-development strategy, but he did not restrict the question to one division or the marketing department. This was everyone's problem to solve.

By the end of 2020, Fox Factory had achieved record quarters for both sales and earnings per share. The outstanding results, said Mike, "reinforced our confidence that we could handle any tactical crisis with strategic initiatives and with a new co-elevating operating system. While day-to-day work was being done, we were still able to implement real collaborative foundational management systems and processes for the future. That was a true testament to the alignment and unprecedented teamwork we were able to adopt within the organization."

Pulling together as an integrated team was the only way to deal with so many crises at once. "We needed to remain incredibly nimble as shifting and new challenges changed daily, from Covid cases to wildfires to social unrest and, eventually, overstretched supply chains," Mike recalled. "In fact, there were many weeks where we battled all the above at the same time. Success was measured both in terms of organizational and enterprise survival and real improvement toward our long-term goals."

We have seen co-elevating teams like the one at Fox Factory create tens of billions of dollars of shareholder value through innovation and transformation, supported by people's stubborn refusal to let each other fail. Keith has coached these same co-elevating behaviors and practices at some of the oldest and most hierarchical *Fortune* 500 companies, at entrepreneurial midmarket brands, and even at fast-growing startups. In all these instances, the highest-performing teams, fueled by co-elevation, were able to uncover unexpected growth and control downside risk. They shared the load of leadership and fought united like a band of brothers and sisters to achieve audacious goals and extraordinary results. Their first step on that journey was to explicitly agree to new behavioral norms for teamwork: to *recontract*.

Recontracting for co-elevation

The work of a true co-elevating leader is to promote a shared sense of responsibility among team members and nurturing a common ethos with which everyone is committed to each other's success. Before the integration of Fox Factory's operations, each product line would rise and fall on its own performance. But to achieve the kind of growth

Mike desired, there would have to be bolder thinking that pushed the leaders of all product lines to seek new ways of collaborating. Product line team members had always had strong accountability and met their goals and commitments. In the face of a crisis, and with their new aspirations for growth, they had to become dedicated to hold each other accountable. Instead of the traditional hub-and-spoke concept of a team, with the leader at the center, co-elevation requires interdependency among team members in the form of candid peer-to-peer support and peer-to-peer accountability. Even when team members are competing for resources or put their opinions first, they can still commit to each other's success as a foundation for mutual support. No one is successful until everyone is successful; the team crosses the finish line together.

The GFTW faculty members noted how naturally teams in crisis fell into many of these highly productive behaviors. Under normal circumstances, however, the best way to achieve this sense of shared commitment is by having the team agree to an explicit social contract for its collaboration. This process is described at length in Keith's previous book, *Leading Without Authority*. The team members need to openly discuss and debate all the desirable attributes of team behavior and then agree to support each other's growth and success in maintaining those behaviors. The transparency of the process and the contractual nature of the agreement make living up to the behavioral standards a serious commitment, even a matter of personal integrity.

Signing an agreement to adhere to specific behaviors may seem a little contrived, because typical collaborative efforts begin with little or no discussion of these issues. That is especially true when all the team members have known each other for years and are colocated. It is seductive to believe that if we are all working in the same space every day, then we all share similar understandings about commitments and accountability. And yet, we have all been in enough dysfunctional collaborations to know this is far from the truth. In any collaboration, a common social contract needs to be negotiated, or a faulty one is likely to be the norm.

Recontracting is especially important with virtual and blended teams, where there will most likely be remote workers who are not equally included. Adding remote team members can encourage the creation of new social norms for high-level collaboration within the organization. If you need an excuse to shake things up, the expansion of virtual and blended teams can give you a chance to be a change agent and seize the opportunity to recontract for a shared team culture of co-elevation and cocreation even better than what existed when the teams were colocated.

For any leader, initiating a candid recontracting discussion begins with a simple exploration of observable behaviors:

1. Which working behaviors need to improve in order for us to achieve our immediate objectives?

2. Which new high-return practices should we adopt to support and sustain our improved collaborative behaviors going forward?

Leaders can then ask the following questions, which are based on the benchmarking survey Ferrazzi Greenlight conducts with teams at the beginning of, during, and at the end of coaching engagements:

1. Does our team have conflict avoidance? Do we challenge the thinking in the room and speak candidly even when it is risky to do so?

2. Does our team have silos? Do we collaborate and create tangible value from the interdependencies that exist between us?

3. Is our team encumbered by hierarchy or control?

4. Are we dedicated to holding each other accountable, doing whatever it takes to cross the finish line together?

5. Are our team members deeply committed to each other, leading with generosity and building caring, trusting, and supportive relationships with one another?

Maintaining psychological safety within the team takes deliberate and focused effort, whether your team members sit next to you at the office or live on the other side of the world. Recontracting goes far beyond the kind of casual relationship-building that occurs among office mates who nod at each other in the hallways and occasionally have lunch together. The contract has the benefit of reminding everyone what the ideal team behaviors are, causing them to reflect personally on where they might be falling short.

When Ferrazzi Greenlight begins work with a team, we ask the team members to rate their team according to twenty-two co-elevating statements. Then, through the coaching process, we survey the members and track the scores on all twenty-two of these statements as indicators of progress. First-rate executive teams at organizations like Fox Factory, Delta Air Lines, General Motors, Verizon, Unilever, Salesforce, and many others have gone through this process to raise their expectations for themselves and to raise their game.

Physical distance is not the main roadblock to co-elevation involving remote workers. The chief problems to be overcome involve strategic distance (a lack of team alignment) operational distance (a lack of well-oiled team process to operationalize the work), and affinity distance (the lack of team members' commitment to one another). Studies show that of these three measures of distance, *affinity distance* has the greatest effect on innovation, trust, learning, and team outcomes.[2] Close the gaps in affinity distance (commitment for each other's success) among your team members, and most of the issues involving the other two dimensions—strategic distance and operational distance—will organically become much more manageable. And in no instance does physical distance register if a team has recontracted for co-elevation.

Leading a co-elevating team through the process of recontracting takes time, courage, and perhaps some coaching, but it should not feel like drudgery. The point of co-elevation is to get everyone striving to be better—better for their own careers and better for each other. It should be a joyous and expressive enterprise. During the height of the pandemic, when stress levels were high and exhaustion was rampant, more teams reported that the members felt more connected and committed to each other than they had ever before. People pulled together and committed to a new set of rules for that moment. Now the open question is, how can we sustain that sense of mutual commitment as a matter of choice, not crisis?

In that sense, co-elevation has much in common with a barn-raising, the Amish tradition in which everyone pitches in selflessly while learning from master crafters directing the work. To the Amish, raising a barn is hardly the sole function of a barn-raising. The gathering is also an opportunity to build relationships and strengthen their shared Amish culture. Some Amish refer to a barn-raising event as a *frolic*, from an Old Dutch word for "merry" or "cheerful."[3] You want your teams to function in the same way. If your collaborations don't feel like frolics, it is likely that some of your teammates don't feel psychologically safe, and your co-elevating team needs to resume its recontracting discussions.

As a critical new leadership art form, co-elevation improves over time and with the help of methods we've researched and identified as high-return practices. In 2020, as we shifted our coaching business to fully remote team coaching, we saw a powerful opportunity to test all these remote and virtual work high-return practices that we'd been developing for more than ten years. We found massive shifts in measurable change across all the teams we were working with—a 79 percent increase in candor, 75 percent increase in development, 46 percent increase in collaboration, and 44 percent increase in accountability.

After working with teams at NI, formerly National Instruments, CEO Eric Starkloff told us, "It was a breakthrough. There's no way we would have been able to react with the sort of speed and get the sort of buy-in we see today." He said that before our coaching, there had been a widespread assumption that *collaborative* and *fast* were at odds with one another when it came to decision-making. "The tangible change has been the ability to escalate and make critical business decisions faster. And [decisions] that stick, because the process is collaborative, and therefore, the buy-in is higher with many more inputs."

High-return practices for collaboration

After the new social contract is agreed to among team members, it's time to initiate a set of practices that support and encourage the new behaviors so they can grow into habits and rituals. Following the lead of Fox Factory, NI, and many others in 2020, here is how you can try some of the best high-return practices that we have identified at Ferrazzi Greenlight and GFTW Institute.

Go to the breakout rooms

Virtual environments require frequent use of breakout rooms as acceleration pods of deeper collaboration. Avoid seeing yourself as the center of your team. Your job is to ask the smart questions and to break the team into smaller groups of two or three people. During each breakout, have everyone take notes in a shared document and then come back to the larger meeting with reports from their group. Even if you do not have time for formal report-outs from each group, the owner of the question will have the benefit later by having access to everyone's written input. Our research shows that teams that operate in this way solve problems faster and get bolder contributions from many diverse voices. That's because people who are conflict-averse are reluctant to share openly in a big room and feel more psychologically safe in breakout rooms of two or three people. Organizational behaviorist Amy Edmondson and her team of researchers at Harvard define psychological safety in four simple dimensions. Team members feel safe under these conditions:

1. When it is permissible to make mistakes

2. When sensitive topics are openly discussed

3. When team members are openly willing to help each other

4. When differences among team members are welcome, that is, when team members feel free to be themselves[4]

All of these factors are enhanced in small groups, where team members feel the safest to speak openly in service of the team, its mission, and each other. People in small groups have more courage to express themselves about difficult questions. They will self-critique and weed out weaker ideas. When groups return to report back, our research institute has found little evidence of dilution of courage or candor—an estimated 15 percent dilution at most. That's because of the power of the intimacy in the breakout rooms. Team members don't want to lose face by watering down their candor when they leave the breakout and rejoin the main group. Commit at least 50 percent of meeting time to work in breakout rooms, and you will see the value of deep candid collaboration radically accelerate.

Practice collaborative problem-solving

All these tools are critical to executing on collaborative problem-solving (CPS), one of most powerful virtual meeting frameworks we know. Developed through many years of coaching *Fortune* 500 executive teams, CPS focuses on a single business-critical question or several of them in a sixty- to ninety-minute meeting. For at least half of the session, the team breaks into small groups of three or four people to discuss the question or questions and report back. The questions could involve how to achieve a specific upside goal or mitigate a specific downside risk. Craft the question carefully so that it's easy to have up-or-down answers. What innovations could we bring to the retail experience? What's most likely to derail us in the next six months? From there, everyone preps by drawing in data and insights from their wider teams. Everyone is also clear on who will make the final decision: who *owns the question*. The question owner gives instant feedback, for example, either a clear "Yes, we will do this," or a "No, and here is why not," or a "Maybe we will look at this and do more research."

The aim is not consensus; it is robust dialogue and an action-oriented conclusion. The most powerful element of CPS is the small-group breakout process, because it encourages candor and diminishes conflict avoidance. When meetings consist mainly of time-wasting report-outs, that's often a symptom of a team struggling with candor and failing to collaborate effectively. CPS can break the logjam and open up the possibility of fewer meetings and more asynchronous collaboration. As later chapters will show, CPS is an essential meeting framework that can be used to accelerate results through every application of radical adaptability.

Cut back on meetings

No matter whether they're in person or online, about one-third of your meetings are an absolute waste of time and energy. Meetings also take a heavy toll on the mental focus of individual team members. Too many meetings during the day is the reason so many people work nights and weekends just to catch up with work that requires unbroken periods of time for deep concentration. At GFTW Institute, we've studied *asynchronous collaboration*, which is a way of using virtual tools to accomplish better and more thoroughly what you might have scheduled a meeting for. *Asynchronous* means doing more work through collaborating through written or recorded form without meeting at the same time. This kind of work allows team members time to express themselves clearly and commit themselves clearly. The keys to successful asynchronous work include (1) simplified, concise communication; (2) clearly identifying the decision-maker for each action item; (3) making every communication transparent to the whole team; (4) being responsive to every communication you receive; and (5) allowing your team time to review the material you share with them.

GitLab and Dropbox are just two of many companies that now have a policy of "asynchronous by default" to encourage team leaders to avoid scheduling meetings. Both companies offer handy guides on etiquette for asynchronous collaboration and writing tips as well.[5] A reasonable goal to shoot for is a 30 percent reduction in meeting hours next month. Start with a conversation that relaxes everyone and arouses empathetic feelings for one another. Go deeper than the superficial small talk you might make at the start of an in-person meeting. With team members scattered at different locations, it's important to warm everyone up to their shared humanity, so they're more than floating faces on a computer screen.

Share the sweet and sour

If you must meet, open meetings with relationship and empathy. Online meetings should always begin with proper respect for everyone's need for connection. For larger meetings, a good way to conjure the spirit of empathy quickly is to begin by asking everyone to share something sweet and something sour in their lives. The sweet could be something simple, like an achievement by your child, or anticipating a friend's visit from out of town. The sour might push people for greater vulnerability, however, to speak of a loved one in the hospital or a spouse having difficulties. Social scientists have long advocated using the power of vulnerability and empathy to bring people together, an idea popularized by best-selling author Brené Brown.[6] During the pandemic, we saw leaders exhibit plenty of vulnerability and authenticity as they struggled with the unpredictable work demands and expressed fears for the health of their loved ones. This sharing bonded us and opened up levels of trust and acceptance that hadn't existed before. Empathy is always of value in an in-person context, but it is absolutely necessary online.

Conduct a personal-professional check-in

With each virtual encounter, whether it's a meeting or a call with someone you have not spoken to for a few days, be sure to do a quick personal-professional check-in at the start. What is really going on personally with you? What is really going on professionally? We add the word *really* because people need to go deeper and focus on our struggles and vulnerabilities, not just on small talk. Effective co-elevation requires team members to have a sense of how everyone is doing, mentally, emotionally, and physically. This goes beyond the sweet-and-sour empathy exercise. You need to understand what's on your teammates' minds if you want to operate at the full potential of your team relationships. Once teammates feel invited to share their lives with each other, miracles can happen out of such conversations—miracles of service and commitment that build lasting, trusting relationships.

Maximize your use of online collaborative tools

The pace of collaboration is quickening as bold ideas become more portable and shareable. A new generation of online apps have greatly improved the capabilities for asynchronous and real-time collaboration among team members. That way, teams can cut back on meetings, or when meetings are necessary, members who missed them can catch up later by watching the video. Look beyond those tools to a new generation of virtual whiteboards and apps for brainstorming and collaboration that make asynchronous collaboration easier and more effective. Many of the new apps offer fast and useful group feedback through polling and survey features borrowed from the world of social media and gaming.

Take candor breaks

Team members who truly care about each other will offer candid criticism to express sincere concern for the good of the team—the essence of co-elevation. But if you ever get the sense that everyone's avoiding the elephant in the room, calling a candor break is the best way to discover what is being held back. Pause the meeting when the time feels right, and ask the team, "What's not being said?" Ask for a candor break, then go into breakout rooms, where everyone addresses that same question. Take notes in each breakout room, then share them with the whole group.

Break through Silos by Teaming Out

The animating principle of co-elevation is what we call *teaming out—* reaching beyond the organizational limits of your team to draw in others to cocreate solutions. During the pandemic, we observed how this dynamic drove companies to blow apart their organizational design and tear up their organization charts to look for bold ideas by teaming out across their businesses. I (Keith) titled my previous book *Leading Without Authority* to point out this shift in the definition of leadership beyond bureaucratic limitations. Everyone is a leader. Everyone is obliged to speak up and step up when the occasion calls for it.

For every leader, teaming out begins with the question *"Who's my team?"* In the new world of work, the answer is not what you've traditionally thought of as your team. Members of your team include whomever you think might be critical to achieving your mission. You must be willing to look beyond organization design and lines of authority and consider the people—inside and outside the organization—who are needed to join you in cocreation.

From there, you must reach out to those people through the three leadership points of *serve*, *care*, and *share*. Ask how you can be of service to them. How can you demonstrate that you care about the mission but also about them? What can you share of your own experience that makes it easier for your associates to connect with you? From all these perspectives, how can you build the bonds of mutual commitment? These are the principles our colleague Rob Whitfield, CEO of Ferrazzi Greenlight, coached into play at Aflac, one of America's leading insurance companies.

Serving, caring, sharing

Virgil Miller is not a man who misses his numbers. President of Aflac Group and executive vice president and chief operating officer of Aflac U.S., Virgil is a former US Marine who was determined to push forward the company's digital transformation.

"I started a digital journey with Aflac years ago," said Virgil, who has studied the science of teams and collaboration. "Our digital transformation has been in flight, and we continue to pilot new tools. But I felt this would be a great time to accelerate and to get people to think differently. To do that, I needed our teams to be pushed and to be challenged and really collaborate more."

At the front line, Aflac's call center was caught between serving internal and external clients—fielding calls from existing customers, the policyholders (typically a benefit administrator at an employer), and sales agents, intermediaries, brokers and agencies, with sales accounting for about a third of incoming calls. The problem was that the call center was part of the operations reporting line, but sales was not. The answer was to break through the silos on the org chart and bring together the sales team and the customer support team in the call center to design digital solutions that worked for both teams. The challenge for both groups was to lead without authority—to show they could collaborate to solve a problem that affected both of them without needing an explicit executive mandate to initiate action.

Digital automation and a new approach to peer-to-peer coaching was the answer. Fifteen of the most digitally advanced sales reps were given the responsibility to transform how the call center was run. They became the vanguard of a digital-first movement. They coached their peers on accessing information through a new set of online training articles, video tutorials, and a conversational artificial intelligence (AI) channel that was spun up in a blistering six weeks. Instead of needing to phone the call center for help, sales agents learned through peer-to-peer support to rely on these new tools. Call and chat volume fell by 40 percent, while there were substantial improvements in agent experience, and in customer experience as well. Annual savings for Aflac, if the program were to be repeated throughout the organization, was estimated at millions of dollars.

The reduced strain on the call center agents has made everyone happier. "There's always been intermittent collaboration between the call center and the sales team," said Nicole Evans, director of customer service center process, innovation, and control. "But since Covid, it has been what I would call a rekindled romance. And it has helped us all better understand the necessity of moving digital, increased our desire to do it, and given us a shared sense of purpose." Put another way: the Covid crisis accelerated transformation for Aflac, not just digitally but culturally. Amid a crisis, Aflac found an opportunity to co-elevate.

"I've been at Aflac [for] twenty-eight years, and I've never seen the level of collaboration and partnership that I'm seeing today," said Blake Voltz, vice president of customer solutions center operations. "It has allowed us to understand the needs of both teams and develop a program that capitalizes on our strengths."

Faculty with GFTW Institute observed a recurring theme in 2020: solutions previously seen as impossible became apparent when people looked beyond the boundaries of their organization and their control. The pandemic forced many to recognize the severe limitations of their organizational hierarchies and how important it is to cut through those limitations in the new world of work.

Earning permission to lead

The most exciting aspect of building strong co-elevating teams in the new world of work is that the process is not exclusive to reporting relationships or confined by organization design. The co-elevating ethos of empathy, generosity, and candor naturally compels the group to expand the boundaries of its reach beyond the tight inner circle. Great teams keep expanding their reach using all the tools and practices discussed so far, putting them to use in expanding the teams' reach far beyond the limitations of their core team members. They team out by redefining the shape and scope of the team according to the mission at hand, not the org chart.

This process of teaming out includes whoever outside the formal team is needed to get the job done. The key is to adopt a leading-without-authority mindset. To achieve this, follow four basic steps to reinvent your team scope and earn permission to lead:

1. *Redefine who your team is.* In the case of Aflac, people had to see beyond their operational authority of the call center to define the solution differently—to digitize the sales organization. Once they did, they saw a way to transform the situation they had struggled with for years, getting squeezed between two customer groups they were desperate to serve with limited resources.

2. *Accept that it is all on you.* Crisis creates audacity and a resourcefulness that is often not seen outside of such extreme circumstances. Post-pandemic, we need to tap into the same resourcefulness as a regular source of inspiration and opportunity, to ignore silos and boundaries, and to team out through co-elevation.

3. *Earn permission to lead.* Remember the three words *serve, care,* and *share.* How can you be of service to a teammate today, for example, giving the sales reps hours of their day back to them? How can you demonstrate that you care by creating and paying for an initiative that would better serve them and their needs? What can you share of your own experience to make it easier for your teammates to be of service to you? How can you express your care as Virgil did, by reaching out and building a relationship with the head of sales to ensure that the call center initiative was seen as it was intended—an improvement in service of the sales organization?

4. *Cocreate the solution with this broader team.* The value of broader inclusion is that the team can find solutions that are not available to those with more limited exposure to the problem at hand. For example, the collaboration between the sales and call center/operations teams at Aflac helped define solutions that would work for both teams.

Hybridize Teamwork for Inclusion and Crowdsourcing

After a few months of using their new remote tools during the pandemic, some organizations truly seized the advantages of engaging teams in a new way. They began to explore how online inclusion and collaboration could fuel innovation at scale. By experimenting with these new tools, global companies like Google, AT&T, and Deutsche Telekom began crowdsourcing bold ideas about product innovation and policy development across employee networks.

Research has shown how this form of inclusion can improve both business growth and employee morale, engagement, and retention. One study concluded, "Because many large companies have pockets of expertise and knowledge scattered across different locations, we have found that harnessing the cognitive diversity within organizations can open up rich new sources of innovation. Indeed, internal crowdsourcing is a particularly effective way for companies to engage younger employees and people working on the front lines."[7]

Survey platforms and other tools to support such rapid and efficient outreach have been around for years. Most, however, had been underutilized as mere one-way broadcast media. Even remote town halls were often produced as noninteractive video presentations. For many companies, it took the pandemic's shift to remote working to reveal the tremendous potential of virtual tools to promote collaboration and inclusion at scale.

Fabian Garcia, CEO of Unilever North America and Mike Clementi, Unilever's head of global people ops and North America head of HR, were two partners in such an innovation. In 2016, they launched a commitment to diversity and inclusion under the banner Every Voice Matters. But it took until 2020, in the throes of the pandemic, for the program to gain true momentum. The year 2020 produced some of the best financial results Unilever North America had ever seen. But Fabian and Mike wondered, how can we sustain the pace of growth and change into 2021 and beyond?

"I think what 2020 did was accelerate what was already there and compress it," Mike explained. "It was a pressure cooker of work. We realized there was no way we were going to repeat the level of ambition with just muscle and sweat equity. We needed to be more precise around the way that we engineered work. We started to then think about 'how do we do it?' and understanding that there isn't the capacity to repeat in 2021 unless we made better choices—it was all about choices. Then it was about getting new thinking and multiple people working on it." And that's where internal crowdsourcing came into play.

Annual planning at Unilever had always cascaded down from leadership. The year's top strategic priorities were chosen and handed down to the next level for execution. But in 2020, Fabian and Mike opted to crowdsource ideas from senior managers (below the executive leadership team) to identify the greatest opportunities for growth and the likely risks they needed to avoid. Crowdsourcing allowed the organization to open the aperture wide for new ideas to flow in. Teams were invited to think strategically and submit ideas that promised enterprise-wide impact, while squads were formed to fine-tune all initiatives. To build a sustainable basis for this work, Unilever built crowdsourcing time into people's daily schedules—making it clear that the work was high priority and high visibility.

"We had some people work in natural teams and some volunteer to be part of the squad for the year ahead," said Mike. "We had very strong engagement [and] new ideas and wrote clear objectives and key results that were signed off by the top team."

From an initial list of more than ninety initiative submissions, six priorities emerged to help Unilever win in 2021. When leaders actively reach beyond their businesses to seek out fresh ideas, listen, and act on the solutions, the benefits stretch beyond the commercial impact of whatever result is put into practice, whatever new product is launched, or whatever service is taken to market. This inclusive approach to collaboration on the most important questions facing the business—its future success and direction—creates an alignment with mission that will filter through the organization. To the evergreen culture question,

"Why are we doing this?" there is no better answer than "I was among the voices that said we should."

Deepen External Partnerships

Faced with a pandemic-driven disruption of traditional go-to-market models and supply chains, many companies seized the opportunity to co-elevate with both customers and suppliers—to reach out and draw them closer in. Virtual tools added speed and scale to such collaborations, allowing businesses to tap new sources of external information and insight that they had never directly engaged with before. These deepened external partnerships, forged in the chaos of the pandemic, have been revealed as an essential collaborative best practice in the new world of work.

At Dow, Inc., the bold, inclusive approach to external partnerships helped make 2020 a year of innovation and transformation. Dan Futter, Dow's chief commercial officer, explained how the business generated 80 percent more leads in 2020 than it had in even its historically best years. Its new digital engagement strategy was the dominant driver of this growth. Prior to 2020, Dow had relied on relationships with existing partners and trade shows to generate business leads. But when the pandemic shut down live events in the first quarter of 2020, Dow had to rethink its customary approach to lead generation.

"If you'd have asked us what we were doing," Dan said, "most people would have said, 'Oh, we're trying to replace what we always did in person.' It was going to be a digital facsimile of the old way of working. By about June, it was, 'Hey, well, this doesn't have to be some pale imitation. This remote-first strategy is different. It gives us opportunities to do things better than we did in the past, and it overcomes some of the limitations of doing things in person.'"

Using digital tools opened up new opportunities for Dow to work with its small customers, the thousands of bench chemists and formulators who use Dow products but who had lacked direct communication with the company.

"What we were able to prove is that digital-first was a great democratizer for us," said Dan. "It meant that we could talk to anybody at any time, irrespective of the gaps between us and how we transacted, and so we suddenly had our know-how and the insights of those customers brought together in a way that had never happened before. It was a superb opportunity for us to get more people at the table."

Market information that used to be filtered through a distribution chain now reaches Dow directly from frontline customers—and at a previously unimagined scale. "Where I used to talk to one chemist at a time, now I'm talking to hundreds at a time," said Dan. "Where I used to not get any insights about the market other than what was fed to me by my distributor, now I can get that direct from the people engaged in the market and the insights that come from it. It's absolutely real, and we're just scratching the surface of where that can get us to."

At Dow, 2020 was truly a year of finding growth through a radical approach to inclusion and collaboration. Instead of exchanging emails, the company is deeply engaged in virtual, synchronous collaboration with its partners, and there is no intention to snap back to old ways of working. Besides opening up new dialogues, digital virtual tools have been used to cocreate solutions in real time with external partners. "I used to have to jump through all sorts of security hurdles to do an external WebEx," Dan recalled. "And we never had shared my team space with customers. We suddenly said, 'Why are we keeping all these security barriers? Let's have a shared program, a team space. We can be sharing stuff with one another twenty-four hours a day around the world. What's the next innovation? What have we just discovered? What have we just tested? What have we just learned?'"

As Anup Sharma, senior vice president, global business services, for LyondellBasell Industries, explained, 2020 was an inflection point for partnership building of this kind: "We have been committed to leveraging this time of disruption to defy the traditional vendor relationship standards in our industry."

One of the world's biggest plastics, chemicals, and refining companies, LyondellBasell joined with Air Products, a global industrial gases business, in a collaborative effort to make one company's off-products become a value generation opportunity for both. From LyondellBasell's perspective, the collaboration spans three key themes: mutual investments, reliability, and sustainability. Each company will execute changes in processes, meetings, and mindsets over time to drive the collaborative relationship throughout the organization—leading to a regular cycle of transformative review.

Rob Whitfield explained how this reframing of a traditional transactional relationship between two organizations in the chemicals industry—sometimes collaborators, sometimes suppliers, sometimes competitors—has found the potential to unlock a 10X opportunity in the future.

"There had been efforts in the past to work more closely together, but the companies were in a coexistence state rather than doubling down on where they could do more together," Rob said. "They were leaving so much on the table when it came to opportunities to innovate around resources. In order to gain 10 percent, they were overlooking opportunities for 10X results." The pandemic prompted a switch to virtual meetings and gave new momentum to collaboration. Conversations that started individually in each firm eventually became team conversations and then cross-company conversations.

External collaboration of this kind is responsible for this book and the enormous amounts of research behind it. Ferrazzi Greenlight was one of many consulting firms that saw its pipelines and projects grind to a screeching halt in the spring of 2020. We recognized the opportunity to dig deeper in our research and to serve and build even deeper relationships for the long term.

For years Keith had partnered with Frank Congiu of LHH as hosts of dinner parties for chief human resources officers. In fact, Frank and Keith hosted one such dinner in Manhattan on March 4, 2020, the night before the first set of lockdowns threw the country into a standstill. Soon afterward, Frank and Keith committed to pull together all the chief human resources officers they had been convening for years and give them a forum to be available for each other during these tumultuous times. Keith reached out to friends and clients at World 50, Dell, Anaplan, Verizon, SAP, EY, Salesforce, and many others to do the same with our respective clients. We would all just serve, with no expectation. A series of virtual roundtables followed in which we discussed the disruption and how we might turn it into an inflection point for future of work. Within months, this group of participants would evolve into what we now call fellows of the GFTW Institute.

We ensured that the early roundtables began on a positive note, and that co-elevation was the objective. Frank recalled, "We always started by asking people to open with what their silver lining was. Participants would share stories about spending more time with their children, not getting on airplanes for the past few months and foreseeable future, getting to know colleagues better by seeing inside their homes and family lives. Once we moved into the call, HR leaders were in a good mindset and ready to share the best practices of what their company was doing and how they were doing it. It turned into a great forum for best-practice sharing."

And the result? Roundtable participants were able to take fresh thinking—rooted in evidence of what was working elsewhere—back to their leadership teams at a time when everyone was feeling stretched. "I have clients that have shown up to the roundtables and others who have not," Frank said. "And overall, I would say the people who have gone outside of their organization and leaned on peers have been more effective. This is the power of crowdsourcing ideas and collaborating with external partners."

Frank added that companies like Synchrony, Wolters Kluwer, and IBM have seen an uptick in their employee engagement scores from practices they learned in these sessions. "That happened in a time when you'd assume that scores might go down," he said. "I'd also say these people show up more connected and interested in general when I meet with them. I suspect they have plenty of external engagement, but they seem to be particularly grateful for the model we have created of deeper sharing and commitment." According to Frank, there was a triple win—for LHH, for clients, and for himself in terms of professional development. "Not necessarily something I learned, but certainly something I confirmed is how important it is to lead with generosity," Frank explained.

This simple, powerful idea of inclusion—reaching out to draw people closer in—ultimately blossomed into the GFTW Institute and this book. You are reading the fruit of a deeper client and partner collaboration coming out of the pandemic.

Expand Your Personal Coaches in a Remote World

Our research showed that the most intimate level of collaborative inclusion that ramped up considerably during the quarantines and social distancing of 2020 was an increase in executives' willingness to open themselves up to each other for advice and counsel. Many leaders evolved personal support networks of advisers and coaches throughout the pandemic. Our discussions at the GFTW Institute told how they reached out more frequently, and in deeper ways, primarily because of the unprecedented need for shared insights, assisted by the virtual tools we all began using and by all the time freed up by the decline in business travel.

On a personal basis, many of us reached out to old friends we'd lost touch with for open, more vulnerable sharing and peer-to-peer coaching. The virtual environment lent itself readily to tapping into advice from peers inside and outside the company, and even outside our industry. We learned to bulletproof our ideas with people we respected and admired and with a more diverse set of individuals—like old friends who had a perspective completely outside our organization's culture. In our own work, we've been blessed that some of our team meetings have been joined by thought-leader friends like Peter Diamandis, Jim Kwik, and Vishen Lakhiani, and in return, we've been honored to join and help their teams.

One powerful lesson granted us by the pandemic is that we can generously serve each other as coaches for learning and development, even if we never see each other in person. Before the pandemic, we might have met serendipitously at a sales conference, for example, or down at the bar at the end of the day, when peers share struggles and stories as they commiserate and problem-solve. When the remote work environment of the pandemic erased these opportunities for informal learning, leaders at some companies stepped up to formalize the kind of learning that had previously happened by chance. With so many employees stressed and time-constrained, there was an urgent need to connect them with organized peer-to-peer coaching resources.

WW (formerly known as Weight Watchers) always prided itself on the power of providing certified coaches in support of members (customers), and members in support of members. As WW evolved its business model along the digital spectrum to offer online coaching and workshops, the company also decided to pilot formal coaching among its new online coaches. Small groups of three coaches met weekly to share coaching struggles and solutions as they journeyed from physical to online coaching. They explored how to make the best of online workshops, how to engage members best online, and how to balance personal responsibilities (like childcare and home education) with coaching responsibilities. The coaching became a formal system for peer-to-peer support and advancement in a new way of working.

At Merrill Lynch, where there had already been the company's robust peer-to-peer Advisor Growth Network, the isolation of the pandemic spawned a peer-moderated semiweekly podcast with three to four thousand of Merrill's financial advisers dialing in weekly. "That's unheard-of," said CEO Andy Sieg, "to have that many advisers stop what they're doing on a regular basis to hear what the firm and their peers have got to say."

The dynamism and free flow of ideas among the leaders at the GFTW Institute has been a grand, ongoing exercise in teaming out—an antidote to the quarantined world, with inclusion as the driving force for innovation and growth. As your co-elevating teamwork takes shape and evolves, you want to keep looking for opportunities to reach outward to draw more people in. It's not enough, however, to lead a dynamic cocreating team into a rigid, hierarchical management structure. These new tools and best practices will not achieve their potential in terms of speed and flexibility if they are controlled by a slow, internally focused bureaucracy. Creating value in the new world of work is defined by team empowerment and customer-centricity—the central principles of agile management, which is the subject of the next chapter.

GUIDING QUESTIONS
How to Compete in the New World of Work

Do we come together as a team with a shared commitment to radical collaboration, and not only in times of crisis?

> The most successful companies ignore organizational structures to ensure that everyone on the team crosses the finish line together. By recontracting with a commitment to co-elevation and employing a set of high-return practices that foster inclusion and collaboration, we can uncover unexpected revenue and risk-mitigation opportunities.

Do we harness innovation and collaboration beyond our team and from all corners of our organization?

> We have known about the wisdom of crowds for centuries. With the widespread use of communication and collaboration technologies, radically inclusive companies systematically cast a wide net across the organization and, in doing so, generate a broader set of innovative ideas and collaboration opportunities.

Do we leverage a broader external ecosystem of customers, vendors, and partners to drive higher levels of collaboration?

With the pandemic, we found ourselves in the trenches together, facing common challenges. As a result, what were once transactional relationships suddenly became deeper and more empathy driven. Radically inclusive companies deepen external partnerships and find opportunities to co-elevate with customers, vendors, and partners—and even competitors.

Lead through Enterprise Agile

Our focus group research at the Go Forward to Work (GFTW) Institute showed how pandemic-disrupted companies, motivated by dire necessity, discovered they could achieve extraordinary results in record time. Within weeks of the pandemic's first travel advisories, Delta Air Lines launched an entirely new Global Cleanliness Division. General Motors, in the space of a single month, retooled its automotive factory lines to manufacture respiratory ventilators. Unilever wasn't even making hand sanitizer in the US market when the pandemic struck. Six weeks later, the company was delivering a new product to stores.

These and many other companies accomplished such feats through a bundle of practices we call *crisis agile*. They tasked self-organizing teams with specific measurable objectives. The teams met frequently to collaborate on overcoming roadblocks. They innovated and cocreated through constant iteration. They sprinted to short-term interim out-comes, then kept reassessing and pivoting toward achieving their objectives. These are all practices emblematic of *agile*, the fast-moving working discipline that originated in the software development field.

The pandemic made the shift toward agile a necessity, not a choice. Delta Air Lines, for instance, had an urgent need to keep its passengers safe by sanitizing its fleet after each flight. The objective was clear and the customer benefit was obvious, but there was no time to devise a solution through normal hierarchical channels. Instead, the decision-making and problem-solving had to be pushed down to the people closest to the work itself—a critical agile principle. And under those con-ditions, agile practices (whether or not they were recognized as such) like self-organization, daily stand-up meetings, and weekly sprints proved to be lifelines. By its nature, agile invites breakthrough innovation, because agile presses every team member to keep asking, who else do we need on this team? How can we create more value? How can this project be better?

"During crises, you'll see managers astonished by how fast their teams can innovate and come up with solutions," said Sarah Elk, coauthor of *Doing Agile Right* with Darrell Rigby and Steve Berez, her colleagues at Bain and Company. In early 2020, I often ran into Sarah and her col-leagues on my book tour for *Leading Without Authority*. Later, she became one of my guides when the GFTW Institute was researching how agile's principles could have a lasting effect in the new world of work.

We found that crisis agile revealed the possibilities of a new radically adaptable way of planning and executing work throughout the orga-nization, all the way up to the C-suite. We're talking about a sustainable bureaucracy-busting approach we call *enterprise agile*. When practicing enterprise agile, all teams from the executive team on down share com-mon agile values. Most teams are self-organizing. They iterate quickly by continuously sharing problems and overcoming roadblocks together, all with the common goal of providing more value to more customers faster and better.

High-Return Practices for Competing in the New World of Work

1. Always put customer value first.
2. Drive team autonomy downward.
3. Lead biweekly sprints toward measurable outcomes.
4. Bulletproof the work through team feedback.
5. Scale to sustain innovation.

Many of those who resorted to crisis-agile methods during the pandemic ended up exhausted by the experience. It would be a mistake, though, to confuse the turmoil of crisis agile with the practice of agile as a deliberate discipline. "With agile," Sarah Elk said, "you can capture that speed of innovation as an ongoing process but without the chaos that comes with crises."

That's the promise of enterprise agile in the new work of work. You shift your leadership approach and delegate responsibility to teams closest to work and closest to the customer. With enterprise agile, every team's job is to innovate and create customer value. Meanwhile, leaders need to give their teams increasing opportunities to take on more and more operational responsibilities through the following high-return practices: First, the teams develop the discipline of putting customer value ahead of other considerations. Then team autonomy is driven downward, setting biweekly sprints toward measurable outcomes. Completed work gets bulletproofed through team feedback. The final step is to scale agile throughout the organization for long-term sustainable innovation.

The previous chapter showed how remote and blended teams require high levels of communication and accountability to achieve radically adaptable collaboration. The same is true for agile teams, but agile teams raise the stakes by combining the best practices of collaboration with their obsessive focus on creating customer value. As a leader, you have the opportunity to set the example for a new agile operating system that achieves radical adaptability through every team in the organization.

During the 2020 period of crisis agile, it was easy to see how agile created value for external customers. Delta provided a clean, safe fleet for its passengers, GM produced ventilators for hospital patients, and Unilever met consumer demand for hand sanitizer. The more subtle and powerful benefit of enterprise agile, however, is how executive teams can change their behavior to serve *internal* customers—other departments and divisions dependent on their work processes. Those internal customers in turn are better able to satisfy the company's external customers. That's how enterprise agile contributes to raising performance, improving overall outcomes, and growing revenues.

Always Put Customer Value First

In March 2020, when state governments began issuing public health orders restricting the numbers of people in stores, Target Corporation, like all retailers, faced a set of totally unforeseen problems. How could Target's thousands of store managers control the flow of shoppers to comply with these rules? Target regards its store customers as its guests. Leaving people waiting in long lines outside your stores in March weather is no way to treat your guests.

Target team leaders from three divisions—the technology, stores, and digital teams—met on a Friday afternoon and decided that an ideal solution would be an app distributed to the mobile devices carried by store team members. To control the flow of shoppers and conform to local health codes, the app would be an improvement on manual clickers, sign-up sheets, and lines of shoppers waiting outside the doors. But could the company develop a single app for all of Target's in-store team members when limits varied greatly from state to state and city? Complicating matters, those limits were changing frequently, sometimes daily. By the following Monday morning, an agile development team at Target was assembled for the task.

"We discussed what lines are like in other spaces," recalled Lindsay Keyser, the product lead on the project. "Is it like a deli counter, the DMV [Department of Motor Vehicles], a restaurant?" The team members eventually settled on the online check-in model for haircutters—one customer goes out, one comes in. They conceived of a mobile app that would be customized to help in-store teams use their handheld devices to manage the numbers of shoppers in their stores.

Software engineering teams ranging in size from three to twenty started work from different ends of the app—one team wrote computer code for the user interface while the other team wrote code for the underlying architecture.

The engineers sometimes stayed on remote calls for hours as they wrote code together and shared ideas. Within a few days, they had something that had begun working. "We were in a store by the following Thursday," said Lindsay. One of the engineers later told her, "I've never shipped something to a store that was developed within a week and a half. It was awesome."

Throughout the effort, the devil was in the details. Arizona's restrictions were particularly stringent, and the stores there required frequent changes. The team tried to give individual stores control over the app, then quickly found that they had to take control back. The agile process proved to be fast and flexible as each new wrinkle came to light. In-store team members gave feedback directly to the development team, which made adjustments, fixed errors, and improved the user experience.

Thanks to agile, the app reached its internal customers with no need for a budget authorization, no resource request awaiting approval from senior management, and no bureaucratic review of any kind. The team was empowered to bring its idea to life.

"It was really fun to start out with no defined mock-up of what the screens would look like," said Lindsay. "There was nothing like that to slow us down. We just put something out there, and if it's confusing, we can improve it. The screens were dynamically configurable, so we could go in and make improvements to the look of the screens, and the changes would show up on devices in every store within ten minutes, without anyone needing to update the app."

The ability of Target's teams to move so fast and flexibly reflects the profound effect agile has on work behaviors and attitudes throughout the company. "There's a culture of flexibility and collaboration by design," said Rich Agostino, Target's chief information security officer and a faculty member of GFTW Institute. The agile mindset—marked by the spirit of optimism, problem-solving, experimentation, and learning from mistakes—has facilitated product innovation and product development and enabled a broader culture of enterprise agility at Target. "Silos cannot exist," said Rich, "because teams are all dependent on one another to operate and cocreate solutions that ultimately deliver great experiences for Target's guests."

After the product launch, engineers from the stores division reviewed real-time user feedback in a series of daily stand-up meetings. They sorted out their needs for fixes, changes, and new features and prioritized them in their backlog of tasks to do. Under traditional management, the app would not have reached this point in weeks or months. There might have been round after round of meetings to determine what should or shouldn't be in the app before people gave their specifications to a tech team, which then might have outsourced the project to a contractor. Under the old way of doing things, the need for the app might have been gone by the time it was ready to launch.

The need for speed is why, as the entire business world has grown increasingly dependent on digital technologies, agile has crept into the management of more and more business processes. In 2017, when Target's stock price was getting hammered by soft revenue growth, the company set a goal of boosting sales of its profitable in-house brands by $10 billion annually. To do that, Target needed to design and launch thirty new brands over the following two and a half years.[1]

There was a problem, though. The launching of new in-house brands was the responsibility of two teams—brand design and legal—and they had never launched more than two new brands in a year. For each new brand, the start-to-finish process normally took eighteen months. Now the two teams had no choice but to switch to an enterprise-agile process that focused on satisfying an important internal customer: Target's retail division, with its urgent need for thirty new in-house brands.

The first thing to be disposed of was the old, linear, bureaucratic processes in which the brand design team would make a formal presentation that the legal team would take weeks to review and respond to. Instead, by working in weekly and biweekly sprints and doing daily stand-up meetings to make constant course corrections all along the way, the cross-functional team of design and legal produced within two years outcomes that would have previously taken ten years or more.

The urgent need to dramatically accelerate slow, hierarchical, bureaucratic work processes is exactly what inspired the creation of agile software development in the first place. Agile emerged in the 1990s as a response to an industrywide crisis: The traditional way of writing software code was failing its customers. Enterprise-level software had gotten so complex that writing new code was taking too long. Developers were releasing software that was obsolete on delivery. Code-writing's reliable old step-by-step *waterfall process*—submitting finished pieces of code for review and approvals through a series of tollgates—was itself obsolete. Agile practices evolved so that software could be updated more easily and more frequently, on an ongoing basis that could meet rapidly changing customer needs.

Now a similar crisis has arrived for business leadership in the new world of work. New technologies are creating opportunities faster than old bureaucratic methods can effectively deal with them. As digital technology becomes a determining factor in the future of almost every industry, enterprise agile becomes the natural operating system for radical adaptability.

Drive Team Autonomy Downward

Enterprise agile produces innovative solutions by continually experimenting and testing toward measurable outcomes. It overcomes bureaucracy-created obstacles for which there are no bureaucratic solutions.

For example, securing company data safely in bureaucratic silos can make that data all but impossible to use and share in ways that would create value for customers. That was the problem confronted by Mariya Filipova at health insurance company Anthem, Inc. in 2017, when she was vice president of Anthem Innovation. Patient data is a powerful source of innovation in medical processes and treatments, but Anthem's data security firewalls and cumbersome governance rules made patient data inaccessible to both hackers and researchers alike.

Mariya and her team took an agile approach to solving the problem of how to share anonymized patient data in ways that guaranteed both patient privacy and company security. The desired outcome would be a fast and reliable experimentation engine, an online "digital sandbox" that would allow researchers and automated machine learning tools to root around inside Anthem's massive data storehouses. The first task? Mariya set out to identify innovative thinkers inside the teams focused on data science, information security, and legal. She challenged each of them with this question: why do you think the sandbox is a bad idea? She and her team noted every concern and objection they heard and then embedded those issues in the project's specific OKRs—the objectives and key results by which they would measure the project's success.

Within three months, Mariya's team unveiled a prototype for the data sandbox that achieved all the security requirements, but users recruited to test the sandbox found it slow and difficult to work with. Over the next six months, some of these initial users were enlisted to help design and build the second version of the sandbox, which worked much better. That new version provided access to seven billion claims over twelve years, and researchers used the data to study the progression of comorbidities (the effects of two medical conditions in one patient) and to identify the best methods for treating breast cancer and preventing its recurrence. Within a year, a new version of the sandbox, with an upgraded user experience, offered research access to an additional twelve million claims.

Results like Anthem's are only possible when teams are iterating and learning on their own, not following directions from on high. Agile proponents often cite this quote from legendary computer pioneer John Tukey: "Far better an approximate answer to the right question, which is often vague, than the exact answer to the wrong question, which can always be made precise."[2]

Everyone knows what it's like to work on ill-conceived projects that fail because the assignment set from on high was to answer the wrong questions. With enterprise agile, the job of every team is to innovate and create customer value. It is not for team members to prove their worth to their supervisors. "When agile is done right, it doesn't mean throwing away control, it means modernizing it," said Rich Agostino. "Not many people will complain about removing processes they find bureaucratic."

Leading with an agile mindset and achieving enterprise agile requires leaders to pull back from micromanaging operations, and spend more time defining the strategic missions that drive their teams. "The principles of agile may seem like a recipe for a poorly controlled environment," said Rich. "I've heard some refer to it as the 'Wild West' because they don't understand it." As Target's chief information security officer, Rich added, "It would be easy for me to be fearful of keeping up with teams releasing code changes daily, experimenting with new technology, and doing away with old control structures like tollgates. But instead of being fearful, I've embraced it as an opportunity to think differently about how to build security agility."

At Target, security agility is achieved in part by giving thousands of developers access to security testing tools that deliver test feedback in minutes. And instead of trying to teach security procedures to the engineers in rigid, scheduled training sessions, Target has made the training continuous through secure coding tournaments and other gamified experiences. Target's approach is a prime example of how leaders give agile teams increasing opportunities to take on more and more operational responsibilities. At Target, all technology teams within the company, not just the cybersecurity team, are accountable for meeting the organization's goals for security.

Stepping back from hands-on control may seem risky, but innovation has always been risky. It takes risk to keep changing your business at the same rate of change experienced by your technologies, your customers, and your industry. Traditionally, command-and-control innovation attempts to reduce risk through deliberative planning before the actual work starts, but that approach just raises the cost of being wrong. Studies have shown that about two-thirds of *Fortune* 500 companies have been forced to abandon their major strategic plans, often at tremendous expense.[3]

By contrast, agile experimentation controls risk through frequent testing and incremental learning. Venture capitalist Fred Wilson of Union Square Ventures reviewed the performance of his portfolio of startups and found that among the failed startups, 80 percent never managed to innovate beyond their original vision for their companies. Among the successful startups, however, two-thirds had found success by discarding whatever founding vision had gotten them funded, because trial and error had led them to a new vision of success.[4] YouTube, for example, originally launched and failed as a video-dating app. Only then did its founders decide to try using their online technology for a wider application.[5]

The agile design of Anthem's digital sandbox is a great example of how agile reduces downside risk while allowing for massive upside gain. The guiding principle for every new feature was to start small but design for scale from the beginning. That way, when something doesn't work well, it can be stopped quickly with a minimum of lost resources. But when something did work well, the process allowed it to be accelerated and scaled much faster than had been done in the past.

"The rate of our transformation as an organization," Mariya wrote in one of her reports, "is directly proportional to the velocity at which we can execute safe business-relevant experiments." Her observation reads like a credo for success in the new world of work.

Lead Biweekly Sprints toward Measurable Outcomes

With enterprise agile, the spirit of experimentation and focus on measurable outcomes opens up all kinds of opportunities for the leadership team to boost its efficacy. You ask more questions and give fewer directions. What are we going to achieve this week? In the next two weeks? How do we move? Where do we pivot? Can we measure the outcome? If not, why not? Asking these questions through bold and fast iteration helps keeps agile teams on track.

The next critical step is executing through frequent one- or two-week sprints. Working this way allows for interim adjustments and pivots to ensure that teams are not drifting off target, the way teams are prone to drift when aimed at monthly or quarterly results. For most situations, two-week sprints are just frequent enough to get substantial work done for a measurable outcome, yet they then allow for adjustments before moving on to the next sprint. For more urgent projects, weekly sprints might be more appropriate. Crisis agile was frequently achieved through weekly sprints.

At the end of the sprint, the team members have a stand-up meeting and a discussion around several questions: What did we achieve? Where are we going? And what do we need from the team and each other? Where are the obstacles and roadblocks? The ability to pivot, from sprint to sprint, is at the heart of agile's effectiveness. You celebrate progress in hitting measurable short-term objectives, and when mistakes and blind alleys occur along the way, the negative impacts are limited because your team is iterating biweekly and meeting frequently, even daily. These simple iterative ways of organizing work can keep your team triangulating sprint after sprint, toward the North Star of the organization's longer-term goals.

Technology teams rely on formalized agile processes for continuous innovation throughout all the systems processes and technologies that support the organization's activities. For example, the customer checkout process at Target is continually maintained and updated by groups of agile cross-functional teams, with each team working on continuous improvement of a separate checkout process function such as scanning, coupon redemption, and payment authorization.

Under the agile process, a senior leader in Target's store operations team "owns" the vision, road map, and feature prioritization for the entire checkout process. That leader partners with the tech team members in a fast-paced, iterative way that includes daily stand-up meetings (sometimes called *scrums*) to prioritize product updates and changes in line with shifts in customer behaviors and preferences.

That's how an agile team is set in motion, with a *noble mission* from a senior executive who defines the customer problem that needs to be solved. At Target, each cross-functional agile team (usually between five and nine people) is assembled, with an *owner* and an agile *coach*, or *scrum master*, assigned to monitor progress and keep the process on track. The team assembles a backlog of tasks and sets a sequence to prioritize the backlog, always according to customer impact and customer value.

At the heart of every successful agile effort is the initial project brief that ensures alignment and speed toward a common goal. These one-page templates, created by an initiative owner, cover outcomes, milestones, resources needed, and impediments. Once the brief is written, you begin on *sprint zero*, where the team works to agree on the brief, challenging all assumptions and getting clear on exactly what is to be delivered and by when.

Once the team is clear on these issues and agrees on the brief, the agile team typically starts its first two-week sprint, pulling from the top of the prioritized backlog and then meeting every morning to discuss what's getting in the way and who needs help. A typical goal is that every two weeks, the team has a working prototype to put in front of customers. Then the team comes together to discuss the next two-week sprint.

David Frazee, vice president of the Corporate Research Systems Lab at Minnesota-based 3M, has been leading dozens of groups of teams doing agile work for more than fifteen years. As someone who began his career in slow, top-down, bureaucratic methods, he speaks of agile in terms of someone who has been through recovery. Once, when giving closing remarks at a three-day agile training event for thirty-five teams, he told them, "You haven't just been trained. You've been through rehab. You are now starting, this minute, to behave differently from here on. Because when you come out of rehab, you can't relapse."

Designing agile work requires breaking down big tasks into smaller tasks that each agile team can take on simultaneously. The art of agile work design, said David, is to make sure that every team assignment is small enough to be quickly achievable, but still big enough to be meaningful.

"Every team needs to do something that matters," David said. "It can't be so big that you're putting some major thing at risk, but it can't be so little that people will scoff and say, 'Well, anyone can do that.'" Agile is a movement in the sense that every agile project is an advertisement for the process. It reflects the value of doing things in this new way.

"You want to size it so that the achievement will be remarkable," he said. "You want people to look at it and say, 'You moved all that earth with just that many people?'"

Agile is inclusive by design and built for teaming out. New employees, however naive and ill prepared they might be, can be dropped right into an agile team, where the team's self-organizing structure naturally helps new team members figure out where they can make immediate contributions. For 3M, this was an unexpected bonus, said David. Agile was introduced at 3M with the expectation that it would increase velocity and productivity. "But what we didn't realize," he said, "is that you can add teams and people to the organization nonstop, essentially at will.

You could take anybody in and just throw them into a team, and they would be assigned a task that's consistent with their competence."

That's a world away from how things used to be at 3M, where a young new employee would first need to be schooled in the bureaucracy of budgets, plans, and projects, "and eventually, once you understand all that, you might be able to contribute and find your little niche."

Before March 2020, when the pandemic sent everyone home to work, daily stand-up meetings for 3M's agile teams were always just that—physically gathering in the office to exchange ideas about the day's work. When those daily stand-ups suddenly became daily remote meetings, a new possibility opened up for company—agile teams no longer needed to be colocated. With 70 percent of 3M's lab employees in the Minnesota headquarters, they had never before considered that they were missing out on the contributions of the other 30 percent of lab employees working on separate teams around the world. The 3M units in Asia and Europe, which had previously integrated their work with the main lab in Minnesota once per month, are now fully involved with 3M's remote and hybrid global agile teams.

"What really happened is that it forced us to treat the global labs as part of our team," he said. "And that was really the breakthrough. Had we not been forced to do that, I would say we'd probably still be thinking of them in terms of, 'Hey, would you check our work and make sure you're OK with it?'"

Bulletproof the Work through Team Feedback

By working in sprints toward customer-centric outcomes, agile gives us a new way of working. Teams move away from an obsession with each member's productivity and go toward a sense of mutual responsibility among the members of the self-organized, cross-functional teams. The presence of people from different departments provides checks and balances throughout the process. Again, the key is to make sure you have all the right stakeholders involved, but if the members of an inter-departmental team cross the finish line together, the group has probably achieved its outcome by proactively addressing the kinds of issues that might have scuttled it if they hadn't been caught in time. We've sometimes heard people call this approach a *premortem*.

Leaders managing agile teams may wonder how they can make sure their people are productive. Without micromanaging outcomes, they want to know how they can make sure people are putting in their best efforts. But here's what most executives *should* ask themselves: how do I make sure my people are working together and working well? This question gets to the heart of how leaders manage and design their organizations for accountability—and the issue certainly transcends how their teams are organized.

The advantage of working in sprints is that in the intervening days—or even hours, depending on the urgency of the project—the team members shoulder the responsibility for deciding what work needs to get done, by whom, and by when. Peer-to-peer accountability of this kind is the overloaded manager's best friend. If you spend your day trying to keep everyone accountable, you're not really leading. You're in the weeds, and you're not doing anyone any favors. In fact, you're probably slowing down your team and your company.

Agile teams should operate so that it isn't any one individual's commitment to meet a goal or complete a project; it is the team's responsibility. This approach is in line with the collaboration commitment to "cross the finish line together." If someone stumbles or runs into problems, another colleague needs to stop, look back, and bring a teammate over. That might mean sharing resources or sharing time, but it's absolutely critical to have a team that shares accountability.

Moving to agile leadership and incorporating sprints gives your teams the *framework* for accountability. But how do you make sure your members are communicating with each other and giving everyone the information they need to hold each other accountable? We recommend a tactic we call *bulletproofing*.

When Ferrazzi Greenlight begins work with an organization, one of the first things we notice during initial audits of team meetings is how much time is consumed by *report-outs*, in which one person after another gives a long-winded account of what they're working on. So many wasted opportunities for true collaboration and problem-solving! That's particularly true with teams where the members are committed to holding one another accountable.

With bulletproofing, the report out becomes a focused presentation. An individual spends fifteen minutes talking about the big projects he or she is tackling, the risks and challenges, and—crucially—what the team can do to help. The team then breaks into small groups of three to constructively discuss the presentation. These breakouts can be as short as ten minutes, but the size of the small group is nonnegotiable. It must be three. If there are more than three people in the breakout, candor goes out the window.

During the breakout, the small groups discuss the following:

- What challenge or risk should we bring to the larger group's attention?

- What innovation or new ideas might be beneficial?

- What help or resources can we offer?

After the breakouts, everyone reconvenes and offers insight. The beauty of bulletproofing is that you've done more than provide the presenter with feedback. You've helped mitigate risk by surfacing all the potential issues that the presenter alone couldn't have foreseen. You get fresh ideas. And above all, you highlight the interdependencies of the group.

Agile teams with clarity of mission and adequate resources are capable of self-organizing and self-managing. The teams decide which approaches, people, and resources will be required to achieve its objectives, and the behavior within the team evolves from authority-centric norms into customer-centric cultures. Accountability runs from each member to the team, and from the team to each member. The team gives feedback on performance—not just the boss. Peer-to-peer accountability on this level is a new muscle that our teams must regularly exercise to fully develop, but once it is unleashed, your colleagues will realize that they need to own one another's success. Only then will they cross the finish line together.

Scale to Sustain Innovation

The prerequisite for a leadership team to scale enterprise agile is to make sure that the team itself is running under agile principles. Are you truly committed to helping people learn by doing? Are you stepping back from control, and are you building trust? Are you letting your teams discover what the customer wants, or are you still trying to dictate your own perceptions of customer desires? Most important, members of your leadership team must operate outside the silos of their functional responsibilities and pull together for the good of the organization.

In *Doing Agile Right*, Sarah Elk and her coauthors single out Dell as an example of agile leadership at the organizational level. By their estimation, Dell does four things that distinguish it from conventional companies:

- *Dell plans through extensive customer input.* Planning is heavily informed by customers, either through direct customer research or by encouraging teams that are closest to customers to suggest elements or improvements.

- *Dell maximizes discretion among its teams.* It sets goals and provides guidance but leaves the *how* to its teams.

- *Dell avoids top-level multitasking.* A lot of C-suites try to do everything at once. At Dell, the leaders sequence initiatives to avoid trying to do too much. According to Sarah, "Dell sets a high value hurdle on its corporate initiatives, such that fewer than a dozen are typically active simultaneously."

- *Dell revisits and updates plans frequently.* Agile is based on testing and experimentation. That requires constant course corrections and continual strategy updates based on what's working for customers and what's not.[6]

In the simplest terms possible, the best way to support agile teams is for the leadership team itself to operate through enterprise agile, with its own biweekly sprints aimed at measurable outcomes and with frequent stand-up meetings, peer-to-peer accountability, and bulletproofing sessions.

Agile's speed and flexibility makes it the ideal radically adaptable approach for the fast-paced changes in the new world of work. Agile limits the downside risks of change and magnifies its upside opportunities. But only the leader can make all the strategic planning and budgeting choices necessary to maximize the impact of agile teams. Agile teams are only as good as your strategy, so as you remove yourself from supervising operations, you need to spend more time and effort than ever to improve the organization's foresight and strategic resilience. When agile gives leaders more room to focus on the much-higher-value tasks that only they can do, agile can become an operating system for disciplined radical adaptability.

There are risks, also, in doing agile wrong. Agile represents an attractive, elegant ideal that, like many business terms, can be abused and stretched out of shape. From the top, there are leaders who will claim "We need to be more agile" as an excuse to lay off middle managers. From the bottom, agile teams lacking peer-to-peer accountability might claim that their so-called agile process is why their work is shoddy, late, or incomplete. Some companies have imposed agile on some of their units as a cost-cutting measure, expecting increased productivity without providing any of the cultural and material supports required in workplaces with a lot of agile teams.

Rich Agostino pointed out that Target reorganized its systems for agility in 2015 and has been investing in its agile learning culture ever since. He credits the early success of agile at Target to the company's support for training in the method. Team members were trained in formal roles as agile coaches and technical coaches to support the transition, and Target opened an agile learning center called Target Dojo, where engineering teams can adopt new skills while working on real-world solutions. Target also promotes the idea of *fifty days of learning* each year for each employee. Employees are expected to spend almost one-fifth of their time learning new skills centered on agile.

"For those that have started down the agile path out of necessity during the pandemic," said Rich, "it's important to know that truly building and sustaining agile requires a culture change over many years." Part of the culture change is in the overall tempo of work itself. The daily stand-ups and biweekly sprints can be a source of stress and anxiety for some. Belonging to several cross-functional teams at once, all working on different projects with different deadlines, can lead to collaborative overload. In the next chapter, we discuss the necessity of building team resilience as an essential part of an agile, collaborative, high-performance work culture.

GUIDING QUESTIONS
How to Compete in the New World of Work

Do our operational teams have the autonomy to experiment their way to fast, breakthrough innovation?

Agile teams allow radically adaptable companies to move much faster to deliver value to end customers when they are not constrained by traditional top-down planning and strategy frameworks. Discrete work sprints, real-time feedback from customers, and frequent and focused stand-up meetings all come together within agile to increase the likelihood that projects reach their full potential and happen within a timeframe that meets the ever-changing demands of the market.

Are our team innovation projects overly vague and ambitious, or do we break down our initiatives into bite-size milestones that can be achieved, celebrated, and built on?

Radically adaptable companies often run multiple, or even dozens of, agile teams that make continuous progress toward meaningful goals. At the end of each biweekly sprint, the output is bullet-proofed for quality by the team and external stakeholders, who also agree on the scope of the next sprint and whether a course correction is necessary to achieve the project brief.

Promote Team Resilience

n October 2020, when Apple CEO Tim Cook shared his outlook on the company's fourth quarter with Wall Street analysts, he gave major credit to *team resilience* for the way Apple's financial performance had exceeded expectations.

"Even though we're apart, it's been obvious this year that around the company, teams and colleagues have been leaning on and counting on each other more than in normal times," he said. "I think that instinct, that resilience has been an essential part of how we have navigated this year."[1]

Psychologists who have studied resilience define it typically as "the process of adapting well in the face of adversity, trauma, tragedy [and threats]."[2] Each individual's capacity for personal resilience is highly dependent on the person's mental and emotional makeup.

The science of team resilience, however, is not so well established. What we have found at Go Forward to Work (GFTW) Institute is that teams' adaptability under adverse conditions has much more to do with healthy team behavioral norms and strong working relationships within those teams. How well a team learns and grows from change under normal conditions is a massive predictor of how resilient that team will be when exposed to extreme and sustained levels of pressure and adversity.

The implication is that in the new world of work, while it's important for the team leader to monitor the team's resilience, the ultimate responsibility for maintaining overall team resilience goes right back to the team members themselves. The whole team must take on the challenge of supporting each other and pulling together when, individually, some members are having a harder time than others in dealing with adversity.

The volatile environment of 2020 pushed employee resilience onto the CEO's agenda, elevating what had been a traditional issue for HR. "It's a good time to be in HR, actually," one HR leader told us in our research. "Finally, our leadership is realizing that our people and their energy matter, and that we in HR are finally being turned to for help in critical business issues."

Aspects of team resilience are built into the working methodologies we've discussed so far. All the best practices of collaboration, inclusion, and agility drive performance through flexibility, iteration, mutual support, and other features that benefit team resilience. High-performing teams are designed to be resilient because team members contract with each other for mutual support through cocreation and co-elevation.

Nonetheless, the fast-paced pivots and other course corrections demanded of high-performing teams can be mentally and physically draining. Events outside the workplace impact every team member differently. To maintain team energy and engagement, we need to lead in ways that boost team resilience while also building reliable structures for mutual support among team members. As a leader, you must take ownership of the resilience of your teams while ensuring that your team members share responsibility for each other's well-being.

Teams succeed or fail together, and through our own behavior, we can either enhance or diminish our teammates' resilience. In the following four steps, we show, first, how to gauge your team's resilience

High-Return Practices for Competing in the New World of Work

1. Diagnose your team's resilience.

2. Employ high-return practices for supporting team resilience.

3. Cocreate solutions for acute stressors.

4. Support mental health for sustainable resilience.

levels and, second, some high-return practices for supporting and encouraging team members to build resilience in the team. Third, we share high-return practices for dealing with acute workplace stressors. And finally, we discuss building a sustainable base of mental health resources that will enable your team to sustain its resilience in the disruptive years to come.

While each of us must take responsibility for our own personal resilience in our lives, resilience in the workplace is best achieved as a team sport. Employee energy is the fuel of any enterprise, and that's especially true at the team level, where there is a direct connection between team energy and team performance. The central role of teams in business success, their interdependency at the heart of value creation, and a belief in the importance of team resilience have all been core principles of Keith's coaching practice for twenty years. Teams need to be understood as living organisms, ones whose functional resilience is critical to every organization's overall health.

Diagnose Your Team's Resilience

We first took note of resilience as a recurring theme during research calls and focus groups the GFTW Institute hosted with members of

World 50, one of our earliest partners. Through the focus group discussions in particular, we heard the clear need for companies to be able to diagnose team stressors and cocreate solutions.

At the time, many of the teams Keith was coaching were severely beaten up by the stress of the pandemic. Their leaders were feeling severely depleted, some with tears in their eyes. When Keith sought out more information about team resilience, however, he discovered that workplace resources are usually oriented more around the mental and emotional well-being of individuals.

At the GFTW Institute, we enlisted the help of WW and Headspace, two of the most prominent and passionate brands in the category of workplace wellness, to conduct more interviews around the phenomenon of team resilience. That's when we discovered that the same relational dynamics that generate high team performance are also critical to the team resilience required to maintain such high performance.

In particular, teams that rated highly for co-elevation were also more resilient. The team members were more able to voice their needs, solve problems quickly and collaboratively, and get to bolder action faster. The team culture was resilient, in that the lack of defensiveness or insecurity among team members permitted those with problems to raise their hands and ask for help.

Next we partnered with LHH's Mary-Clare Race and Taryn Marie Stejskal, founder and chief resilience officer at the Resilience Leadership Institute. Our intention was to develop new insights on team-based resilience that would complement all the great work being done on personal resilience, such as Carol Dweck's growth mindset research. We took note of observable actions and behaviors within teams when assessing resilience (as opposed to trying to measure individual thinking and attitudes) and determined that the following team behaviors are the most reliable diagnostic indicators of team resilience.

- *Performance:* Is the team achieving its targets? One of the clearest measures of resilience is whether a team can complete what needs to be done and take the hills that have been set as objectives. Are deadlines being missed? Is the quality of work suffering, or are normal key performance indicators moving in the wrong direction?

- *Candor:* This key indicator of team efficacy is also an important indicator of team resilience. Are team members able to have open and honest dialogue and feedback with each other? The members of nonresilient teams cannot speak truth to each other or collectively identify and decrypt the challenges they face. A lack of candor reflects a lack of trust, a signature of a breakdown in resilience. Instead of candor, people denigrate each other in whispers or offer leaders unsolicited, unflattering reviews of team members. In its worst manifestations, you may have team members bullying or controlling others.

- *Resourcefulness:* When faced with challenges or problems, do your team members build creative and effective solutions together? Resourceful teams devote their energy to solutions and remain focused on outcomes, regardless of external conditions. Teams lacking in resilience tend to waste time dwelling on the unfairness of a task or complaining about the amount of work needed to find a solution. They will wallow in doubt about the purpose of the task, while more resilient teams will express those doubts, work through them, and then develop solutions at a much higher velocity.

- *Compassion and empathy:* Do your team members truly care for each other and share both successes and failures? Resilient teams are made of members who care deeply and genuinely about each other. It is impossible to marshal the collective resilience of a team if there is an absence of care or a lack of commitment to sharing equally in both successes and failures. Resilience is often expressed in deep commitment to co-elevating the team rather than seeking individual recognition or success.

- *Humility and vulnerability:* Can your team members ask for and accept help from other team members? Teams that lack resilience struggle to admit when a problem has become intractable, and the members hesitate to ask for help either from someone else on the team or from someone else in the organization. Problems tend to become hidden, and responsibility for finding solutions obscured.

- *Productive perseverance:* Can your team change its heading but maintain its goal? What Taryn describes as productive perseverance is the capacity to adjust and fluidly navigate between maintaining the mission and shifting in a new direction. Teams without resilience struggle to change course when circumstances demand it and stick rigidly to a plan, or they change course and lose sight of their goal.

- *Grati-osity:* Can your team reflect with *grati-osity*, that is, with gratitude and generosity? Taryn coined this word to describe an ability to combine gratitude and generosity. The gratitude comes in when teams reflect to see the good in the challenge and how it changed them for the better, even if they wouldn't have chosen it. The generosity is in sharing these stories openly, rather than simply doling out advice, so that others may learn from the experience. Teams without resilience avoid reflection or default to blame.

- *Positive intent:* Is your team's mindset to assume best intent? This final behavior is a mindset or perspective: remember to assume positive intent across team members. Individuals may be undergoing personal problems or experiencing stress in ways you may not understand. By believing that your team is doing the best it can, you can communicate support, patience, and empathy. Rather than assuming a team member didn't complete a task, ask if you might have missed an email or a document, or ask how you can collaborate with or support the individual.

A great way for a team to monitor its resilience levels is to run a form of this diagnostic at a monthly meeting through CPS (collaborative problem-solving). Imagine a two-stage CPS, beginning by compiling a list of the stressors facing the business, then a second stage to collaborate at speed to define practical solutions. Adapting CPS to the team resilience diagnostic in this way makes the most of CPS's baked-in benefits—full team engagement with ownership of team problems and their cocreated solutions.

Employ High-Return Practices for Supporting Team Resilience

As a leader, try thinking about resilience as if there's a little dial in the middle of each team member's forehead. The dial measures energy and engagement levels, and it's your job to make sure the dial is on a high setting or to help turn it up. For the sake of team resilience in the new world of work, monitoring each other's energy levels is everyone's job now. Teams that stayed together best during the trying times of 2020 were those in which leaders shared the responsibility with all team members to help keep each other's dials on full charge.

But every individual on a team is different, each with a distinctive personal response to the stressors shared by the whole team. Jan Bruce, CEO and cofounder of the resilience-training software meQuilibrium, points out research suggesting that individuals with talent for creativity and innovation—those most likely to be engaged in strategically important projects—are also among those at the highest risk of burnout in the workplace. And yet those are the people we need to count among our most resilient.

Raising the overall level of team resilience requires a level of self-awareness and empathy that may not come naturally to all team members. Leaders must assess the state of their teams, identify weak spots, and then deliver strategies that will help team members break down barriers and build foundations of trust, transparency, and self-awareness. Our research on high-return practices has identified the following leadership behaviors that deliver the best results for team resilience.

Commit to building each other's resilience

The essence of co-elevation is that we commit to each other's growth through adversity. Use the team recontracting process described in chapter 2 to ensure that team resilience is a fundamental part of the explicit social contract for team behavior. Discuss all the desirable attributes of team resilience, and agree to support each other's growth and success in maintaining these behaviors. Make sure the contract establishes unambiguous expectations around team unity and peer-to-peer support. If someone is struggling, the entire team is contracted to help. If the team ever seems indifferent to someone's struggle, remind the members of the contract and your expectations.

Provide positive feedback, which matters more than ever

Fast and frequent feedback is an important factor in all collaborative and agile work processes. Sustaining team resilience requires that the fast and frequent feedback be framed in positive terms.

Remote and hybrid teamwork adds a level of challenge on this point. Managers must be conscious and deliberate about giving positive reinforcement that used to be given more casually in person. For instance, it's easy to forget to acknowledge an employee after a Zoom presentation, when that employee disappears from a screen. Remote and hybrid teamwork demand this extra level of mindfulness.

Remote and hybrid teamwork also requires open and transparent communication, delivered frequently. At our WW session, AEG's Bill Martin shared that all through the pandemic, he sent out regular messages letting people know their jobs were safe for that quarter, to ease anxiety around job security. That's not a bad practice for *any* quarter in any year.

Share your story; own your challenges

Professional growth and development for your teams should include exercises that build team resilience. To build trust and honesty, leaders must facilitate the process of encouraging team members to express their fears and describe their relationship challenges and then canvass the team for solutions. Use CPS in a space of psychological safety to encourage everyone to map out their life's journey (highs and lows) and then to share highlights with the other members of the team. For example, a facilitator can ask each team member to express their feelings about the state of the team and assess the team's problems as they see them. The facilitator should encourage team members to own their part in any existing problems and ensure that everyone gets an equal say.

Use independent observers

Resilient leaders invite outside experts to offer an objective perspective on team dynamics and other issues. Bring in a coach for team resilience. Doing so can help team members embrace frank assessments of their work.

Show that you care

Leaders have to regularly demonstrate that they are genuinely interested in the progress the team is making; they can ask probing questions to understand the underlying issues that affect team resilience. But asking is only half the equation: resilient leaders must also listen carefully to the answers they get from team members. This is where a resilience deficit will be revealed.

Enforce break times

Minutes, hours, or days away from the office (or computer, as the case may be) is often just what the doctor ordered. Anything from blocking off a ten- to thirty-minute break to taking those PTO days you have earned can be a real boon to your mental health.

"It's important right now for employers to encourage people to go on vacation, whether or not they physically go anywhere," said clinical psychologist Sera Lavelle, of NY Health Hypnosis & Integrative Therapy. "It's been pretty well researched that more vacation time leads to more productivity, more work–life balance, and in the long run, makes people less likely to burn out and less likely to get sick."

Managers should be encouraging their employees to block off break times or incorporate no-meeting times. At Grey Horse Communications, a PR and communications agency based in New York City, leaders put an event on the whole team's calendar at 3 p.m. every day in the spring to remind people to have a break, go outside, and take a walk. Tom Spahr, vice president of talent management and development at The Home Depot, shared that the company encourages forty-five-minute meetings as well as "walking meetings"—going on a walk while you have your meeting on the phone.

But clearly, it is not enough to express the expectation that your team will demonstrate resilience in these troubled times; you must build it from the ground up and then put in place measures to replenish resilience constantly. Think of team resilience as though it were a battery that needs regular recharging to restore its energy levels. Teams that put in place measures to do that will find that they are better equipped and—more importantly—willing to undertake any challenge.

Hire for resilience

As we grow in our understanding of team resilience, individual resilience will become an increasingly sought-after attribute in the hiring and promotion process. When given two or three equally qualified job candidates, try asking each interviewee to recall a challenging situation they had to deal with, and then listen for how they tell the story. Did they take responsibility for solving the problem? Did they ask for help and demonstrate a resourceful attitude? Or do they shift the blame? As they tell the story, listen for all the key diagnostic behaviors for team resilience. Listen for compassion, humility, gratitude, generosity. Ask each applicant what they learned from this experience. The level of resilience in each personality will reveal itself. When it's time to make a hiring decision, you may find that the candidate with the lesser skill levels might have the most to contribute to team resilience. Those skills can always be taught later, and people with high levels of resilience tend to be exceptionally receptive to learning new things.

Cocreate Solutions for Acute Stressors

The pandemic was three months old in June 2020 when Laura Chambers, a former eBay and Airbnb exec, accepted a new position as CEO of Willow, a well-funded and thriving Silicon Valley femtech startup.

Less than two weeks into the job, Laura recognized how much her new team was struggling. Through a series of remote one-on-one conversations, she heard them describe their day-to-day juggling acts, balancing work with personal and family obligations at home. All expressed similar passion for the company's mission—to help bring joy to motherhood—but their struggles varied widely: loneliness, cramped quarters, social isolation. With day-care centers and schools closed indefinitely, parenting issues also varied with the ages and numbers of children stranded at home with the team members.

"It was clear that we needed to do something to support the team," Laura recalled. Having come from larger companies with established wellness budgets and staffing, she knew that her little startup would require a different approach. "I wanted to find scrappy solutions that really helped solve the core problems but didn't require unsustainable cash or huge teams to execute. And I wasn't going to be able to design a one-size-fits-all solution. I needed to get bottom-up ideas and find solutions that were really flexible for individuals' situations."

The search for solutions led Laura to team out and crowdsource ideas from across the organization. In a series of virtual group meetings, Willow's team members diagnosed distinct points of stress and problem areas and then started cocreating solutions around them.

One example to emerge was Project Thrive, a series of online classes like yoga and breath work and coaching/therapy circles. Another idea, to reduce time-management stress, resulted in a system of scheduled "purple blocks," where team members were celebrated for setting aside guilt-free time on their calendars for home activities—working out, taking a walk, helping children with schoolwork—and ignoring emails, texts, and phone calls.

Then, in January 2021, Willow greeted the New Year with a Change Your Habits challenge, in which team members encouraged each other to pick a couple new habits and check in on each other for accountability. "On an individual basis," Laura wrote in her New Year's message, "doing this work with my team has helped me learn to apply strategies of resilience and self-compassion, which has helped me cope with a difficult year."

Through our own research, we discovered that the larger organizations seemed to have less to offer at the onset of the pandemic than did startups like Willow and other smaller organizations. Generic workforce wellness programs were found wanting, in part because they did not reflect the reality of leaders' approach to their own jobs. Progressive HR organizations would design wellness programs, and individuals would take advantage of afternoon nap break rooms or yoga classes while leaders would work foot-to-the-floor through weekends, answering messages 24/7. That is what you did if you wanted to get through the crisis.

The pandemic highlighted the need for thoughtful leaders to first identify and isolate the unique sources of stress in organizations and develop a plan to mitigate each of them. We observed organizations generate several innovative solutions to address different stressors through 2020.

Performance-pressure fatigue

Kristin Rand, vice president of corporate compliance and global risk at Moderna, described the added sense of responsibility and pressure felt by the biotech company's employees who worked so hard to develop and manufacture Moderna's Covid-19 vaccine. "On a daily basis, we give our all. . . . My colleagues are constantly thinking about the needs of people around the world."

Hundreds of new employees, including Rand, have joined Moderna's ranks over the past year. "Providing resources and opportunity for people to feel heard and alleviate stress—by encouraging open dialogue and time away—is paramount. Moderna's CEO and leadership team have been committed to taking specific actions like avoiding Friday afternoon or weekend meetings and have made a mindfulness and meditation app available to all employees," she said.

Isolation fatigue and team bonding

Working from home is here to stay. It's practical and efficient, and people like it. Gartner research from July 2020 found that 82 percent of organizations will let employees continue to work remotely at least some of the time.[3] Many companies have found success using group chat platforms such as Slack, Yammer, or Microsoft Teams to create a community around parenting for high school students, exercise videos, posting baby pictures, and celebrating birthdays. It's nice to have those places to connect and share, but great leaders do more than that to support team resilience.

For example, the quick temperature check before meetings is a resilience-building exercise that's similar to the high-return practices for collaboration, like the sweet-and-sour exercise and the personal-professional check-in. Leaders need to adapt these kinds of tools to their teams' needs at any given time. Prior to the pandemic, Krystal Zell, the chief customer officer at The Home Depot, always started her staff meetings by asking everyone to share their anxiety level on a one-to-ten scale. Over time, individual group members established their own baseline readings, so, for example, if Phil typically ranked his anxiety at a five and then he came in one day at a seven or eight, the team members knew Phil needed their help.

"I loved this system," said Krystal, "because my direct reports started helping each other in ways you don't normally see in staff meetings when everyone would just go around and talk about what they're doing." As 2020 wore on, the anxiety question got a little old, so Krystal made her kickoff queries more specific to what people were working through, such as, "What's top of mind this week?" and "What's causing you to lose sleep?"

Lack of healthy routines

One common problem with working from home is a lack of structure in the workday, which leads many to neglect making time for personal care and exercise. Some companies encouraged workers to turn the thirty or forty minutes they might otherwise have spent commuting into scheduled time for healthy juice breaks, yoga stretches, or other physical activity. Tim Patno, vice president of sales at WW Health Solutions, has made a point of providing information on wellness tools and tips on healthy habits, such as turning meetings into what he calls learning walks, and "just being of value" to client prospects in difficult times. For some, that has meant "taking contracting talks off the table," but it has also allowed his teams to get closer to the organizations considering wellness and nutrition programs as employee benefits—yielding deeper partnerships as a result.

Support Mental Health for Sustainable Resilience

Studies by the World Health Organization estimate that 264 million people globally suffer from depression, with many of them also suffering from anxiety, costing the world economy an estimated $1 trillion annually in lost productivity.[4]

We all have some stress and anxiety in our lives. The sign of mental health is when one or more specific stresses or anxieties don't debilitate us. Clinical psychologist Sera Lavelle said, "When a person is mentally well, their anxiety or stress is no longer impeding their ability to function."

The pandemic created a spike in workplace mental health issues. An April 2020 survey by mental health provider Ginger showed that nearly seven in ten employees ranked the Covid-19 pandemic as the most stressful time period of their entire professional careers. Some 88 percent of workers reported experiencing moderate to extreme stress, with 62 percent of them reporting at least one hour a day in lost productivity because of Covid-19-related stress, and 32 percent reporting the loss of more than two hours per day.[5]

The pandemic raised general awareness of the importance of mental health in the workplace. At the GFTW Institute, we want to help elevate the issue further. In partnership with Headspace, we've launched a significant ongoing study of mental health in the new world of work with the intention of identifying more high-return practices for addressing the issue.

Here are some of the most important areas where support for mental health is proven to build team resilience.

Management and C-suite behavior modeling

All the training in the world won't help if organizational leaders do not model the right kind of behavior. As managers and executives, you also have lots of stress. So how do you handle it? Do you speak openly with your team about your stressors? Do you block off break periods or mention you're going for a walk or doing a ten-minute meditation to blow off steam? When your team sees and hears these types of behaviors, it gives them permission to take care of their mental health, too. Conversely, if you never take time off, answer emails at 1 a.m., and refuse to discuss stress factors with your employees, you'll create a stigma around taking care of mental health.

You can reduce stigma by talking openly and making sure your staff understands all the mental health benefits on offer by your company. Show your staff that wellness is a priority by being supportive of employees' needs and disabilities and showing empathy for their struggles.

The pandemic turned our work–life balance upside down: we had to work from home, often with other family members present in the house simultaneously (some of whom are also working); longer work hours often became the norm from home; and parents struggled to be responsible for homeschooling children at the same time. It was rough. Senior leadership learned that we needed to promote a positive work–life balance by encouraging employees to put themselves and their families first—and displaying that same behavior.

At our WW focus group session, Tom Spahr of The Home Depot shared that his leaders emphasized a "take care of you first" message to help associates feel that they have permission to be flexible with their time and have a better work–life integration. The leaders actively checked in on associates and encouraged them to schedule homeschooling breaks on their calendar—and followed up when they didn't see it on the calendars.

Resilience training

Resiliency is important for all the staff, from the C-suite to managers to lower-level employees, and specialized training can benefit everyone. HR consulting firm LHH provides solutions for resilience via formal coaching for employees. Also available virtually on its Ezra app, the coaching allows managers and others to seek advice, support, and an improved skill set, allowing for more resilience overall.

Happify Health, a digital platform that claims to decrease anxiety and depression and increase resilience by 20 percent, is currently part of the benefits package at several companies, including Humana, Cigna, and Interior Architects (IA). The platform offers its users more than sixty different training tracks, each four weeks in length and targeting various mental health issues. For example, one is called Beat Burnout and Build Resilience. There are also more than three thousand science-backed activities and games, guided meditations, and community capabilities to encourage connection and support, all designed to reduce stress and enhance resilience.

Management training for mental health support

To attain a solid backbone of mental wellness, management needs to be on board. We can't cut corners on training the upper levels to understand the causes of anxiety, stress, and depression; to learn how to recognize symptoms in employees; and to discover solutions to combat these issues and increase overall wellness and satisfaction in their teams. For example, ID360, which has coached and trained individuals and teams at such companies as Marriott, Microsoft, and American Airlines, offers customized managerial training programs, including one around best behaviors regarding mental wellness in the workplace.

Mind Share Partners focuses entirely on wellness in the workplace and offers various types of sessions and training. Tech company New Relic did a manager training series with Mind Share on how to support mental wellness in the workplace. After the training, 92 percent of the managers reported feeling more comfortable talking about mental health at work. They also reported having a better understanding of how to create a mentally healthy work culture and of how to support a struggling employee.

Just before the pandemic hit in February 2020, Verizon Media worked with Mind Share on an executive session with Verizon Media's CEO, Guru Gowrappan, the executive team, and the extended leadership team. On March 24, Gowrappan tweeted about the session: "It was an incredible workshop about how to cultivate and facilitate a culture of openness, honesty and transparency to destigmatize mental health. In hindsight, the training came at a crucial moment—before life as we know it was transformed by #COVID19. Supporting yourself, your teams, your friends, and your family is essential for all of us to get through this together. Only together do we move #ForwardTogether."

Meditation and mindfulness

Keith first met CeCe Morken, now CEO of Headspace, the popular meditation app, during a research session that our GFTW team was hosting with the World 50 group. He was impressed by her insights on mindfulness and was not surprised to learn that at Headspace, every all-hands meeting starts with a brief meditation session.

"It's helpful for everyone who's presenting," said CeCe, who left a top job at Intuit in Dallas to join the Headspace team in Santa Monica, California. "Deep breathing makes you more relaxed, and you do a better job." More than a thousand companies provide Headspace as a benefit to their employees. During 2020, the company's partnership requests (bulk deals in which organizations pay for all their employees' use of the app) increased sixfold.

Many companies come to Headspace with the expectation of lowering their health-care costs, because improved mental health leads to better overall physical health. But Headspace has found that the greatest benefit comes from improved employee engagement. "Our level of anxiety and the demands on our resilience affects our attitude at work, how productive we are, how much time we might miss, and how we talk about our employer," CeCe explained. "If you're taking care of the wholeness of the person, especially the mind, you're improving everything that you brought them on board to do."

Support of this kind improves people's voices externally, which helps in building a company's reputation and attracting great talent. Adobe, which provides employees with free access to Headspace, knew it scored a success when it saw high adoption rates, noting that Headspace outperformed many of Adobe's other wellness initiatives. "Many people already knew what Headspace was," said Sara Torres, Adobe's global well-being strategist, "and they were excited to download it. It's been our shiny penny." Farmers Insurance began offering Headspace as a pilot after some examiners experienced increased anxiety in responding to policyholders who had lost everything in the 2019 Paradise fires in California. When the pandemic hit, Farmers quickly jumped to offering the app companywide. Since January 2021, about half of the company's employees downloaded the app, coinciding with an uptick in net promoter scores measuring employee loyalty and satisfaction.

The high levels of shared mental stress brought on by the pandemic and recession broke down some of the stigmas attached to mental health issues. "It's becoming part of the normal conversation," CeCe said. "When leaders and CEOs talk about the stress that they're dealing with and the things that they're doing to help deal with that stress, it makes it OK for other employees to talk about it."

The science around mindfulness is still evolving, but it points to benefits beyond alleviating stress. "When you're better tuned in to yourself, you can be better tuned in to people around you," she said. "People in meetings will feel better if you're more focused. You're also likely to make clearer decisions because you're not thinking about the email that you just got."

CeCe and her leadership team have introduced weekly alternating "no-meeting Fridays" and "Mind Days"—essentially a companywide day of self-care. Nine out of ten employees say they have improved focus and delivery, and the same proportion of managers say their team morale is up since the policy started. "The reason that we have stress and anxiety is we either worry about what we just did, or we worry about what's to come," she said. "Set those aside and focus on right now."

Counseling and therapy

Psychotherapy will always be a cornerstone of mental health, and companies that make it easy for their employers to access therapy—ideally at little or no cost—reap the benefits of mentally well, productive staff. While insurance coverage for therapy should be a given, it's important to destigmatize therapy and counseling and ensure that staff is not shamed for using it.

The digital space has also embraced counseling, with virtual therapy more popular than ever. A growing ecosystem of apps is becoming part of the benefits package at companies like Pinterest, Stitch Fix, Sephora, Zynga, Cleary Gottlieb, Starbucks, and eBay—offering employees access to a range of mental wellness self-care tools, mental health coaching, evidence-based therapy, medication management, critical incident support, manager training, onsite therapy, and work–life services.

"Because we suddenly all had to be at home, digital tools became uniquely positioned to serve the needs of folks who can't go someplace in person," said Paula Wilbourne, cofounder and chief science officer of Sibly. At IA, an employee-owned global design firm, mixing digital on-demand counseling with regular monthly sessions generated strong engagement and positive feedback. "Having a strong support system is imperative to ensure that our minds stay healthy and nourished," said Brenda Plechaty, IA director of HR.

Apps like Yammer can facilitate group conversation outside of work topics. At a GFTW focus group on wellness hosted by WW, Bill Martin, chief information officer of AEG, shared that his company started offering listening sessions around various topics, including racial justice. Aside from speaking with licensed therapists and psychologists the ability to talk openly and comfortably about what's causing us anxiety can go a long way. Offering listening sessions and panel discussions around current anxiety-producing issues, such as racial injustice, climate change, and the election encouraged employees to feel at ease discussing their anxieties and foster an empathetic environment within the company's culture.

Connection between physical wellness and mental wellness

The link between good physical and mental health is undeniable. Ensuring that we are physically and mentally healthy allows for a holistic approach to our daily wellness; it's the reason why programs like WW have incorporated mental wellness tools for their members. WW has also released additional mental health content for members such as "5-Minute Coaching," which provides practical guides and techniques that complement existing mindset content offered to members.

Unilever, GE, Deloitte, PayPal, and other companies offer WW and Gympass as a benefit to their employees, giving them a boost to both their mental and their physical wellness. WW offers its members curated meditations from Headspace and has launched a new pillar focused on sleep for myWW+, with tools like sleep tracking, sleep playlists, and science-backed strategies for better sleep. And when the lockdown started, the company added more on-demand content related to coping with the stress of the pandemic.

"We provided a much-needed community connection by transforming thousands of physical workshops to virtual workshops in just six days so members could see, hear, and learn from WW coaches and other members," said Gary Foster, chief scientific officer at WW. For every problem that threatens team resilience, we need to keep asking, how do we engineer a solution? As the GFTW Institute partners with Headspace, LHH, WW, and others to move the science of team resilience forward, we invite you to join us, because the science of resilience needs to be operating in the forefront of every leader's thinking.

The importance of self-reliant team resilience will continue to grow as a linchpin to success in radical adaptability, because the new world of work is characterized by teams of teams working within networks of networks. The role of leadership, in turn, must move away from supervising and micromanaging the work currently underway and move toward developing strategies that determine what work should be done next—next month, next year, and beyond.

After collaboration, agility, and resilience, the fourth major radically adaptable leadership competency is foresight—the skill of seeing around corners. Foresight is the topic of the next chapter.

GUIDING QUESTIONS
How to Compete in the New World of Work

Does our team culture celebrate and support employee resilience?

Radically adaptable companies monitor and maintain high resilience much like a critical battery that needs to stay charged, whether in times of crisis or not. Our leaders invest in the physical and emotional well-being of employees and work to ensure that interpersonal dynamics do not erode team energy levels. Our leaders are vulnerable enough to articulate their own fears and anxieties and can model resilience through their own work habits.

Do we proactively diagnose specific stressors that erode resilience?

Radically adaptable companies use surveys, regular check-ins, and performance assessments to diagnose issues and implement initiatives to keep the team's battery charged. High-return practices like candor breaks and energy-level check-ins are effective at diagnosing overall team resilience.

Do we co-elevate as a team to ensure that we own each other's mental and physical well-being?

The best performing team members own each other's successes, which is a core premise of co-elevation. Shared accountability for every team member's resilience is prioritized.

Develop Active Foresight

R adically adaptable teams are capable of planning for the future, even when the future is unknowable. And they do this by developing a foresight muscle that proactively detects early signals of change and responds swiftly to them.

Starting in December 2019, Rick Ambrose was getting signals that the Covid-19 outbreak in China might pose a greater threat of spreading to North America than government officials were letting on. As the head of Denver-based Lockheed Martin Space, Rick felt he couldn't risk leaving the future to fate. With twenty-two thousand employees in his care, not to mention the company's essential role in national security and space exploration, there was simply too much at stake. His team builds and launches satellites, manages human space flight, develops strategic defense systems, and explores the solar system with interplanetary spacecraft. When your job requires you to have impeccable clean-room standards for developing space systems that don't contaminate outer space with earthborn organisms, you pay a lot of attention to small microbes that may randomly pop up out of nowhere and snow-ball into a global pandemic.

Rick had both a formal and an informal detection process, which gave him critical insights on the pervasive uncertainty of the moment and potential scenarios for the future. Everything his team did between late January 2020 and mid-March 2020, when nationwide lockdowns began, exemplified the process of how to detect forthcoming problems, and create preparedness—not only to mitigate threats but also to capture opportunities, which all crises invariably present.

Formally, Rick received a daily internal summary of all the world's news that is relevant to Lockheed Martin, including any mentions of the company in traditional media or social media. This daily briefing is akin to the presidential daily briefing that the American president receives every morning from the national security team about potential daily major threats around the world. Rick's daily briefing monitors regulatory developments, policy changes, competitive movements, and other potential threats. But it didn't include infectious disease news.

To fill this gap, Rick started actively seeking information about the novel coronavirus, reading reports from around the world and sampling what was happening internationally before the health situation spiked in the United States. He followed an Icelandic travel blog, which detailed how Iceland started testing and screening for Covid-positive patients in late January, a full month before the first Icelandic patient was even diagnosed! And he began speaking regularly with Lockheed Martin colleagues located abroad in Asia and Europe. Working in different business units, they served as listening posts as they faced the pandemic before it arrived in America. One of his counterparts ran a parallel space business unit in Korea, and Rick spoke with her constantly to understand how coronavirus-related lockdowns were impacting her business.

On the final Saturday of January 2020, while the official US government line was that there was little to worry about, Rick sprang into action, deciding he had to prepare his company for the kind of stay-at-home order decreed earlier that week in Wuhan, China—ground zero for the new coronavirus pandemic. He called Mark Stewart, his head

High-Return Practices for Competing in the New World of Work

1. Detect threats and opportunities.

2. Assess and prioritize signals.

3. Respond and plan possible scenarios.

4. Foster a culture of continuous learning.

of operations, and told him, "I need you to pay 150 percent attention to this now."

The two reviewed their ongoing and upcoming projects, including a major exercise that was scheduled for October, when his team would rendezvous a satellite with an asteroid. It was a run-through test that would require almost fifty Lockheed Martin personnel to spend a day squeezed into a command center designed for about twenty people. Could the exercise proceed on schedule with all those employees working remotely? Would the National Aeronautics and Space Administration (NASA), the client, even approve of such a drastic change in procedure?

Later that same day, Mark wanted to understand what the greatest pressure on his staff would be in the event of a pandemic, so he reached out and visited a friend who runs operations at a local hospital. His friend told him that the hospital was preparing for the worst and Mark was advised to do the same. On his way out of the hospital, his friend gave Mark a box containing a surgical gown, an N95 mask, and a portable respirator and said, "Make as many of these as you can."

Mark gathered his team, and they quickly compiled an action plan. Engineering teams got to work figuring out how they could design and affordably produce personal protective equipment. Both Mark and Rick figured that if they could pursue deep space work and land a satellite on an asteroid millions of miles away from earth, their team could certainly work effectively remotely from home for a few weeks. So they also put in an order for two thousand computer monitors that employees could take home with them in the event of a quarantine. And within a week, Lockheed Martin Space used its decades of expertise as a leading industrial manufacturer with experience in next-generation materials to start manufacturing disposable hospital gowns, face masks, and face shields.

Over the following six weeks, Rick and Mark activated their leadership team to pandemic-proof Lockheed Martin Space to the highest standard possible. "We had monitored what was happening globally," Rick said, "and we knew the situation could be dire in America, so we took immediate action." On March 11, when the World Health Organization declared a global pandemic, Rick's team was fully prepared and ready for this new work-from-home reality.

At the time, there was hopeful speculation that the crisis would pass in a few months, but Rick's intelligence told him otherwise. "I knew we needed to hunker down for the long haul," he recalled. "My goal was to figure out how to come out stronger than any of our competitors at the end of the pandemic and continue serving our clients and the nation." With all of American industry reeling, Rick foresaw that only the best-prepared players could adapt to the hardships ahead and turn this crisis into an opportunity. He had huge business goals for 2020, and he couldn't let a pandemic get in the way.

Using these signals and assessments, Rick and his team put their foresight to work and committed company resources to tackle threats that were foreseeable but not at all certain. They took calculated risks to prepare for a pandemic because they correctly assessed that being unprepared might have unacceptable consequences and that being prepared presented powerful competitive advantages. And thanks to the foresight and bias for action of the Lockheed Martin Space team, the satellite and asteroid rendezvous slated for October 2020 took place as scheduled, along with ten satellite launches that year, all of which reached orbit successfully and on time. The division thrived during what was a horrible year for industry generally and became positioned for future success.

What lessons can you take from Rick Ambrose at Lockheed Martin Space and use to develop your own foresight skills? The key to his foresight success was his systematically looking for and detecting early warning signs—signals that could snowball and disrupt his business—and responding proactively to turn a crisis into an opportunity. Lockheed Martin Space succeeded because Rick's team had the foresight to plan for the novel coronavirus by (1) proactively detecting what was happening under the radar around the world, (2) assessing potential implications to their business, and (3) developing possible courses of actions under different plausible futures.

The late great management guru Peter Drucker said that much of the future is obvious, that all you need to do is "look out the window and see what's *visible but not yet seen*."[1] The pandemic was just that—a well-understood threat for which virtually no one was prepared. Its arrival revealed years of lazy thinking and shortsightedness about a subject of vital and growing importance to everyone—the future. The pandemic exposed the enormous danger of ignoring future risks and opportunities that are already visible to us but *still not yet seen*. This chapter offers you a systematic four-step process for how to "see" around corners and lead your team with radical adaptability to win, regardless of what shocks the future may bring, whether technological, geopolitical, economic, or biological.

The purpose of foresight is to identify what you need to do today in order to succeed tomorrow. In the words of Stanford futurist Paul Saffo, "The goal of forecasting is not to predict the future, but to tell you what you need to know to take meaningful action in the present."[2] Nobody knows what the future will hold exactly—the future is multiple and not linear. But through foresight, we can increase our team's adaptability muscle, plan for possible future states, and act proactively to thrive.

The discipline of foresight has been around a long time, and elements of foresight or similar practices have been part of strategic planning in one form or another. But the truth is, most companies don't incorporate foresight tools into their everyday practice and workflow. And as a result, many missed the threat posed by the pandemic, even though it was right in front of them all along. But some teams thrived in the pandemic because, like Lockheed Martin Space and others we'll meet later in this chapter, they had foresight as part of their core competency. Even among the most established companies, the *consistent* practice of foresight is rare. Survey research says that only about 25 percent of all *Fortune* 500 companies have some form of foresight practice or expertise in their executive ranks.[3]

To be sure, a comprehensive foresight practice takes time, dedication, and resources. It needs to be spearheaded by senior leaders throughout the organization, and most executives don't allocate time to this. When times are good, foresight gets pushed to the back burner. But you can't let that happen in a future full of volatility and uncertainty! Foresight is critical to radical adaptability. It helps you see around corners to predict potential shifts and gives your team the courage to be as brave as ten-year-old Tilly Smith to plan for potential business tsunamis. Without foresight, your team will struggle to compete in this new world of work. This chapter will teach you how to build foresight as a key competency throughout your organization so that everyone on your team can crowdsource risk intelligence and plan for the future.

In our research, we found very few companies that were truly prepared for a global pandemic. Most were caught flat-footed and spent months gamely playing catch-up with a catastrophe that had been foretold for almost two decades. Back in 2007, the *Harvard Business Review* ran a special section called "Preparing for a Pandemic," predicting that the global spread of a highly contagious virus "would become the single greatest threat to business continuity and could remain so for up to 18 months."[4] In 2015, Bill Gates gave a TED talk seen by millions; he warned that "if anything kills over ten million people in the next few decades, it's most likely to be a highly infectious virus rather than a war. Not missiles, but microbes."[5]

A thorough foresight practice involves answering three important questions: (1) What is the portfolio of risks and opportunities that we face? (2) What implications do they have for our business, both downside and upside? (3) How should we plan and create internal readiness to mitigate external threats and capture opportunities in response?

Consider an example everyone is familiar with—the weather. We don't know with 100 percent accuracy what the weather will be in four weeks' time. Yes, we have many years of seasonal data and a general understanding, but not certitude. We have a better awareness of next week's weather and even better knowledge of tomorrow's. This knowledge is based on large data sets about what has happened in the past and our consistent scanning of the atmosphere to see how the weather is likely to change in the coming days.

So if you know it's likely to rain tomorrow, what do you do in response? You would most likely postpone washing your car today, you would make sure all your windows are closed before you go to sleep tonight, and you might even change your social plans for tomorrow. We can forecast the risk of rain because we have empirical data and complex models. But the more distant future is different: it isn't predictable, because we don't have analytical models to understand the full range of outcomes for things *we can't yet see*. This is where developing plausible future scenarios comes in handy. It helps you see things that aren't yet visible.

In foresight, we see the future in a similar way to how weather forecasters predict the path of hurricanes—through the lens of a *cone of plausibility*. The center line of the cone, where the hurricane is now, is the most likely path forward and is the baseline future. The outer areas of the cone are plausible places the hurricane may travel to, but with less likelihood. These are called *plausible futures*. As the hurricane gets closer to land, the cone narrows and gives observers a better appreciation of what's likely to happen and how to respond.

In a world where the churn of change keeps bringing the future forward at an ever-faster pace, radically adaptable leadership requires us to integrate the practice of foresight into our daily operations so we can give our organizations the flexibility to thrive no matter what weather the future brings. We need to proactively reframe how we see the future so that we not only detect and assess possible changes on the horizon but also prepare for them. It's a process that makes our teams smarter, stronger, more resilient, and more radically adaptable.

Planning the future is hard, but it's a teachable skill. It's equal parts art, science, and judgment, and our goal is to help you develop this leadership competence to compete and win in a new world of work. Leo Tilman, a thought leader on foresight and a faculty member at GFTW, said that radically adaptable leaders must pursue a "concerted fight for risk intelligence"—namely, anything that can disrupt your business, from regulatory policy and external market and environmental changes to new technologies and new competitors. Far from passively listening to the overwhelming noise of information, this "fight for risk intelligence" is most effective when it involves the entire organization in an ongoing, systematic, and properly resourced foresight process.[6] We recognize that not all companies have the same resources to devote to a comprehensive foresight practice, but every leader, at every level of the organization, can incorporate three foresight tools into everyday practice to help their teams see around corners.

The first step is *detecting* early warning signals that indicate change. A signal is something that can impact your business, similar to how radar picks up incoming airplane signals. The second step involves *assessing* the likely impact of these signals on your organization. And the third step is proactively *responding* to the most plausible future scenarios.[7]

Detect Threats and Opportunities

When the executive team members at Lockheed Martin Space scanned the environment to detect the risks posed by Covid-19, they had two questions in mind: (1) What is our decision-making horizon? (2) What critical assumptions are we making about our business and the nature of its environment?

Establishing a time horizon for detecting signals is critical, as you would make different preparations if the hurricane were three weeks away rather than one day away. And so we need to establish the time frame of expected change to train our eyes to see and our ears to hear the *right* early signals. Start by picking a horizon that is relevant to your organization. We recommend two time frames: one short term, within a year, and one longer term, within five years. But once we start thinking about very long-term horizons, uncertainty increases, so we must treat any long-term projections with a grain of salt.

The second question is also paramount—what assumptions are you making about your business and its operating environment? This will help you consider alternative factors and scenarios that may truly impact your business but that you may not be paying attention to yet. What assumptions about your revenue sources, business model, culture, and human capital do you take for granted? What would happen if they proved dramatically off base? Would you be prepared to decisively change your tactics and strategies if your assumptions were incorrect? Leo Tilman suggests asking yourself, "Are we focusing our attention on the right targets? Are we scanning the horizon broadly and vigilantly enough?"

For instance, revenues in the professional sports industry are largely dependent on the assumption that games attract thousands of ticket buyers. That was a reliable assumption for decades, until March 11, 2020, when the National Basketball Association suspended the rest of its season and when all professional sports shut down shortly thereafter. And yet, only one professional sports organization in the world—England's Wimbledon tennis tournament—had the foresight to carry pandemic insurance. In fact, Wimbledon had been covered by pandemic insurance for the previous seventeen years.[8] Its governing board had long ago detected the devastating threat that a pandemic would pose to its finances. The board assessed the threat as an unacceptable risk and took measures to mitigate that risk—all while improving its brand equity and reputation in the process.

Reflecting on your company's basic assumptions can bring to light areas of both vulnerability and opportunity. Probing the underlying assumptions of your industry is a proven pathway to innovation, groundbreaking strategies, and marketplace distinction. One great way to test your assumptions is to state the opposite assumption of what you hold to be true, and look for early warning signals that may confirm or reject this opposite assumption. Another approach to test assumptions is to look for something everyone knows to be true—or rather, *thinks* they know to be true—and offer a service that *removes* the validity of that assumption.

The online shoe retailer Zappos built an enormous fan base by defying the common assumption that shoes are difficult to sell online because customers prefer to try shoes on before buying them. Founder Nick Swinmurn figured out that if Zappos could offer unlimited returns with no questions asked, shoppers would flock to the site's vast selection of sizes, brands, and styles. Most investors assumed that offering unlimited product returns was not a sustainable policy, but one big investor saw past that assumption—the late great Tony Hsieh, who would eventually become the company's CEO. By discarding what had been a common assumption about online shoe sales, Zappos's foresight gave it a first-mover advantage that has proved impossible to overcome ever since.[9]

Most major industry disruptions can often be viewed this way, as failures of foresight by incumbent companies unable or unwilling to recognize their own critical assumptions—and by the victories of the disruptors to question and capitalize on the wrong assumptions by others. Uber and its smartphone app undermined the taxi industry's assumption that customers seeking rides would always need to call into a central dispatcher. PayPal flourished because the banks and credit card companies assumed they were already fulfilling customer needs for privacy and convenience in a world of rapidly growing e-commerce. Airbnb has become the dominant force in hospitality, where executives always assumed that bed-and-breakfasts could never grow beyond a tiny niche market in their industry.

The same dynamic shows up time and again. In every industry, big and small, you'll find a lack of foresight and rigid assumptions among established players who are losing market share to bold, nimble, tech-savvy challengers. How can you push your team to not make the same mistake? How can you avoid letting your company be a sitting duck? Which side of that equation do you want to be on? The stakes could hardly be higher to win in this new world of work.

Detection is a team sport

Detecting, gathering, and evaluating risk intelligence is a team effort because no *one* person can keep a close watch on all the macro forces that will shape your future operating environment. "Risk intelligence should be considered an existential new kind of organizational competence," Leo Tilman said. "When everyone can think holistically about risk and uncertainty, and when they can speak to each other and share ideas about risk in rigorous common terms, it helps the organization make better decisions in alleviating threats and exploiting opportunities." Leo advocates engaging the *entire* organization "out to its very edges" in the detection and assessment of relevant information about the major forces shaping the future.

By integrating foresight so thoroughly into your operations, you can help raise everyone's awareness that disruptive change may be right around the corner and that it's part of everyone's job to proactively and creatively look around those corners. Leading a radically adaptable organization requires every leader at every level to participate in an active, ongoing discussion about what the future may hold and what the organization can, should, and must do about it this year, this month, this week, and this day.

To incorporate foresight tools sustainably into your strategy, you need to train everyone on your team to scan and detect the various signals of change. Some companies establish dedicated foresight task forces, and while this is a worthy approach, task forces often feel transitory and have end dates. Instead, we advocate that learning the basics of foresight should be part of everyone's job so that foresight reinforces your team's radical adaptability muscle.

At the vast majority of companies, it was no one's job to monitor the risk of a deadly global pandemic or a potential geopolitical conflict. For this reason, it might be beneficial to add external advisers or other thought partners to your team to help you address the unknown unknowns. Developing a foresight capability provides your team with a chance to cultivate intelligence gathering and detecting capabilities in areas where you previously had little or no exposure and will help your entire team to see the company's business activities in terms of their exposure to future change.

Step by STEEP

How do you begin to scan and detect change? Five macro forces will shape the operating environment of every organization: sociological, technological, economic, environmental, and political (STEEP). STEEP analyses can help you gain insight into how an uncertain future may evolve and can help you identify assumptions about the macro environment of your business.

- *Sociological:* Mainly refers to demographic and other societal changes that might affect consumer demand in your industry. It's why toy manufacturers are mindful of changes in birth rates and why carmakers are concerned that record-high percentages of teenagers aren't bothering to get driver's licenses in the age of car sharing and ride hailing.

- *Technological:* Includes all the developments in disruptive technologies, including robotics, information technologies, energy generation, and materials science. The slightest shift in any of these technologies could open new, unforeseen opportunities or create new, unexpected threats within your industry.

- *Economic:* Refers to the business cycle's ebb and flow; shifts in interest rates, the stock market, and the labor market; and trends in consumer confidence indicators.

- *Environmental:* Includes not only short-term elements that may impact your business or supply chains (like hurricanes or outbreaks of contagion) but also long-term climate change and prospects for future access to natural resources.

- *Political:* Includes trends in government regulations, taxation rates, import tariffs, labor laws, treaties, international alliances, and overall stability in domestic politics and politics in nations wherever your company has offices, customers, and critical suppliers.

Depending on your business and industry, some of the STEEP factors may be more relevant than others, and that's OK. It's not a strict formula that you have to probe all five factors; it's more of a guide for potential variables.

In your existing team, divide everyone into five equal subgroups, and assign them to one of the five STEEP categories. Some team members may already have responsibilities related to emerging developments in a few of these categories—a lobbyist who looks out for government affairs, the chief information officer who keeps up with technology, and so on. So pay special attention to maximizing diversity of thought and experience within each of the STEEP subgroups so that each subgroup gets the benefit of different ideas, different functional roles, and different perspectives within your team and organization.

You might ask, how do we teach our team members to detect signals? We recommend starting by looking at history as a guide to better understand the future. And consider asking your subgroups to develop answers to some of these questions: What previous significant events in the recent history of whichever STEEP factor the subgroup is considering created a sudden transition from one era to another? How did that change impact your business or industry? What were the variables in that change? In light of your best understanding, what is the current trend for this factor? Do you think these variables will change linearly in the near term? Or are the changes in the variables cyclical, seasonal, generational, exponential, or orthogonal?

To aid your team's STEEP subgroups, we recommend building a virtual network of experts who can help with your team's thinking every month. Doing so entails following the most prominent strategists, risk experts, and futurists with domain expertise in the various STEEP categories. For example, Marc Goodman, founder of the Future Crimes Institute and a former futurist in residence with the FBI, is very knowledgeable on threats from cybercrime and the perils of "surveillance capitalism." Nicolas Berggruen and his Berggruen Institute offer imaginative insights about the nexus between business and democracy. Nouriel Roubini, a professor of economics at New York University, predicted the housing crash of the Great Recession and has thoughtful ideas on how the future of finance may evolve. Ramez Naam is someone to watch if your business's future is tied to energy production. For years he has been tracking the steady decline in solar energy costs and estimates that oil and natural gas power plants will be uncompetitive with solar installations by 2030. And Leo Tilman and his firm are leaders in fostering risk intelligence and strategic agility at leading companies and investors across numerous industries. These are just a few suggestions, as there are countless other great domain experts to follow in each of the STEEP categories, including in your own industry. So don't forget to ask yourself, "Who in our industry is well known for looking to the future?"

Your team's STEEP subgroups should be researching the experts in their areas, following them on social media, and going even deeper by attending their conferences or thought leadership events, if possible. If you're fortunate enough to interact with these experts in person, ask them explicitly how they think the future of their domain might impact your business or industry directly. Are there academic research centers that study your STEEP category? If so, find the relevant fellows or academics who work there, contact them, and develop an ongoing relationship so you can learn about their work, their research, and their forthcoming publications. Your job as a leader is to challenge your team to identify early signals through the STEEP subgroups, and the best way they can do this is to read widely and research new pathways by talking to experts, including those outside the mainstream. The edges of any domain are where you'll be likely to find the most avant-garde thinking in your STEEP category—and likely indicators of future change. These wildcards at the edge may currently reside below general public awareness, but they may also be highly influential in niche communities, and their existence may portend possible futures.

For example, back in 2009, the US Department of Homeland Security issued a warning to law enforcement about a growing threat of domestic terror from military veterans returning home and joining white nationalist groups. That controversial report was, like the pandemic predictions, visible but largely unnoticed. However, if you knew where to look, it was clear that the growing ranks of white supremacy memes and organizing activities were growing online, for example, on internet message boards like 4chan.com in the mid-2010s. Fast-forward to 2020–2021, and these activities finally reached public awareness, like the tip of an iceberg finally cresting above sea level.

The point is that early adopters of provocative viewpoints (in each of the STEEP domains and even in your industry) are a good indicator of potential change. If you pay attention to what they represent before they hit public consciousness, you might be able to exploit a competitive advantage or be first to avoid a serious level of risk.

Finally, task your team's STEEP subgroups to present a five-minute update on any relevant signals in their domain at your team's existing monthly meeting, so that your team can detect signals and decide on and plan the future. To prepare for this very brief update, ask your team to communicate asynchronously through online communication channels (e.g., Slack or WhatsApp), and use collaborative problem-solving (CPS) to informally discuss signals, threats, and opportunities they foresee in their STEEP category. Ask them to consider this question: does something that has happened in the macro environment have ambiguous meaning for our business? It could be a new product in your industry, a new law, or a report on labor supply. Encourage your team members to explore it further in the subgroup through informal communication channels so they can dive deeper into the potential signal, clear up potential ambiguity, and be ready to present to your broader team every month.

This STEEP detection exercise helps create a clearer picture of what Leo Tilman calls your organization's *portfolio of risks*. In the next step, which we'll describe below, your team will collaboratively assess the importance of these signals on the firm and then decide on appropriate risk mitigation and offensive strategies, which Leo calls *the upside of risk*.

Assess and Prioritize Signals

The Fusion Resilience Center at Morgan Stanley is a massive machine-learning-assisted operation that helps detect and assess threats to the investment bank and its customers from cyberattacks, fraud, terrorism, natural disasters, geopolitical unrest, and even infectious diseases and pandemics. Established in 2017 in response to rising cybercrime activity, the center initially focused on safeguarding the bank by detecting threats in real time, assessing their importance, and prioritizing a response. Every day, the center would pore through reams of data and feed it through proprietary analytics to filter the noise from the signals, displaying the results on a massive visualization wall with hundreds of monitors, similar to a very large risk radar screen or a sci-fi supercomputer on the set of a futuristic spy-thriller movie. By the end of 2019, the center's work had expanded to detecting any threats that could disrupt the bank's business, and it became the Fusion Resilience Center.

The Center was headed by West Point graduate Jen Easterly, a retired military intelligence officer who spent three tours of duty helping to take down terror networks in Iraq and Afghanistan. Prior to joining Morgan Stanley, she served for three years as a special assistant to the president at the National Security Council. (She has since returned to government, confirmed by the US Senate in July 2021 as director of the Department of Homeland Security's Cybersecurity and Infrastructure Security Agency.)

When China locked down the central Chinese city of Wuhan on January 23, 2020, Jen and her team started preparing for the pandemic to arrive in America. Morgan Stanley has a China operation and headquarters in Hong Kong, and the Fusion Resilience Center began to receive worrying data coming out of Asia. Less than two weeks later, the center had built a model predicting worst-case scenarios if the pandemic in China were to go global, using data from public health authorities, universities like Johns Hopkins, and other sources. By following trends in Asia and Europe and synthesizing numerous inputs, the center continuously assessed the pandemic's threat level and advised the bank's leadership day-by-day about how it should respond.

For all its massive technical sophistication, the Fusion Resilience Center still relies on human decision-making in assessing threats and prioritizing responses. Each threat is categorized algorithmically and presented to staff, who then make human-in-the-loop decisions on threat validity. The human team's job is to look at all the data and assess which threats necessitate immediate action, which suggest further investigation, and which are false positives that could be ignored. While the detection phase is largely automated through data inputs and algorithms help flag risk, only human staff can make collective recommendations on what the bank should do next and where to deploy actual resources and financial assets.

To get the risk assessment and action plan recommendations correct, Jen created an approach to systematically crowdsource intelligence and feed that data into the Fusion Center's algorithms. She invited a network of problem solvers that she had established both inside her team and broadly throughout the bank to interpret the Fusion Center's algorithmic assessments, prioritize risks and make recommendations to the bank's leadership.

By mid-March, when virus infection rates began to spike in New York City, the Fusion Resilience Center's forecasts predicted that employees would probably need to work from home during a public health emergency, and the bank's leadership had already made a critical decision to distribute secure technology to every employee in the United

States. So when President Trump declared a national emergency on March 13 and banned all non–Americans from entering the United States from Europe, pandemonium broke out in corporate America. But Morgan Stanley was ready for this new era of the future of work and didn't miss a beat. Over the next nine months, Morgan Stanley had a breakout financial year. The Fusion Center's focus on detecting early warning signals and correctly assessing risk and opportunity played a central role in the firm's stellar performance.

An assessment matrix

Your organization probably doesn't have complex algorithms to flag risk or a matrix-like data visualization room like the Fusion Resilience Center to show your entire portfolio of risks or, in Leo Tilman's words, your *enterprise risk radar*. But you can use similar methodology to assess the downside risk and upside opportunity of change signals through your existing teams.

The chief output of your team's STEEP subgroups is to develop and maintain a continuous and sustainable risk radar for your organization, which, as we explained earlier, should be done at your monthly team meetings. Just like a weather radar, your risk radar displays both the near-term and far-term change signals and monitors their impact on your organization, even if they are not being actively managed. These signals may be plainly visible to outsiders but may not yet be evident in your everyday operations.

And as with weather radar, you can use risk radar to estimate both the likelihood and the impact of potential threats. When a hurricane is visible a thousand miles away on weather radar, forecasters estimate a range of possibilities for its future strength and location. Risk radar works in a similar way. It visualizes the company's entire portfolio of risks and uncertainties, and when this information is accessible to every-one on the team on a digital whiteboard, it enhances everyone's under-standing of what concerns are most important in the company's future.

"This focuses the fight for risk intelligence and planning throughout the firm," Leo explained.

For most organizations, if you ask your team to review signals on the risk radar and report on new developments through their STEEP subgroups, you'll be able to easily prioritize the environmental changes related to each of your risk factors. At your monthly team meeting, you should ask your team two questions: First, what is the *likelihood* of this signal? And second, what is the *impact* of this signal on our business? Retired GE vice chair (and current Nike board member) Beth Comstock eloquently sums up the importance of these questions: "What answers to these questions do we need to have before we can remove this signal from our worry list?" At your monthly team meeting, ask your team to plot each detected signal on a simple two-by-two assessment matrix based on perceived business threat (figure 5-1). Majority vote rules in these exercises, so whichever quadrant of the matrix gets the most votes for a signal, classify that signal in that quadrant. You'll see that the top right quadrant (number 2) classifies signals as having a combination of high likelihood and high impact. For any signal in this quadrant, you'll want to immediately begin a scenario response plan, which we'll later describe further. For the other quadrants, you can

FIGURE 5-1

Risk radar

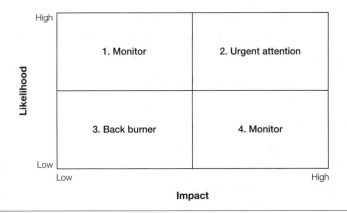

either monitor them before developing a scenario plan or put the signal on the back burner if both the likelihood and the impact of a signal are low. The goal is to use CPS to crowdsource the team's assessment of the various signals so that you know which ones to focus on *now* versus later.

This is certainly a condensed exercise in risk assessment but one that every team can deploy sustainably in its day-to-day workflow and one that every leader must master to make each team radically adaptable for the future. For some multivariable signals, you may find it useful to bring in external thought partners or advisers to your monthly team meetings. Or you might even consider partnering with an outside risk intelligence firm like Tilman & Company to undertake a comprehensive exercise. But this DIY foresight exercise is one that you can rinse and repeat with any signal from your detection phase; you can use it to develop an internal assessment of risks that can then inform your planning and response.

The importance of iteration

Remember that your risk radar is only as good as your team's ability to identify new data and analyze it on a regular and timely basis. Detection is not a once-and-done proposition. The future always changes in reaction to what's happening now. Detection and scanning is a constant exercise. So you have to keep your foresight model continuously updated as a living document; it's not enough to do it once a year and forget about it. We believe it's critical that you schedule a foresight update in your monthly team meeting—even if it is limited to a half hour—to discuss external threats and opportunities. And so the STEEP exercise is designed to provide your team with a tool to easily and constantly do that. Through this detection and assessment exercise, your team can identify vital intelligence about emerging trends and use CPS to prioritize actions and decide how to proceed, practices we'll discuss in the final step of foresight. This builds your team's capacity for radical adaptability and will help you compete and win in the new world of work.

Respond and Plan Possible Scenarios

On March 8, 2020, Santa Clara County, in the San Francisco Bay Area, declared the nation's first countywide stay-at-home order to combat the coronavirus pandemic and closed all nonessential businesses. Jonathan Becher, president of the parent organization that owns the San Jose Sharks hockey team, convened his leadership team to discuss what it would do now that the hockey season had been suspended and ticket revenue would be zero for the foreseeable future.

Facing the most extreme uncertainty of his professional career, Jonathan resorted to his early training in systems engineering. He figured that if he broke down the uncertainties facing the hockey team into their underlying elements, then each assumption could be tested by building out scenarios for possible futures and that the exercise just might point him to some options not previously considered. He tasked his team members with developing detailed action plans for the most likely future scenarios, so that if one or another future scenario came to fruition, they wouldn't be caught flat-footed. They could focus on executing the already-in-place scenario action plan.

Becher and his team considered a wide spectrum of plausible scenarios—some hopeful, some manageable, some catastrophic. What if no fans are allowed inside the stadium for all of 2020? What would happen if only the corporate suites are occupied? What if fans are allowed, but the franchise has to test everyone for the coronavirus before they enter the arena?

Jonathan's team identified thirty scenarios that could plausibly play out in 2020, and the group generated a one-page document describing each of them. In late spring, the leadership team ranked the top five most likely scenarios through CPS and fleshed them out into longer five-page operating documents. Eventually, the most likely scenario was developed into a forty-plus-page action plan, which guided Jonathan and his team through the rest of the year and into 2021, when the Sharks were set to play an entire season with no fans in attendance. Despite the utility of scenario planning, the exercise wasn't foolproof. One scenario they did not consider was that Santa Clara County wouldn't let them enter their own building and practice on the rink, even without any fans in the building. So for the first two months of the 2021 season, the team had to relocate to Arizona, where such restrictions weren't in place. They never considered that the San Jose Sharks would have to play home games in Arizona!

Scenarios are defined as plausible stories that create a bias for deliberate action. In the assessment step during your monthly team meeting, any signal that was voted to be in quadrant 2—representing high impact and high likelihood—needs to undergo a scenario planning exercise so that your organization can prepare proactively for what the future may bring. Each scenario describes an *alternative* version of the future, using a different assumption, even though all the scenarios refer to the same underlying information. Once again, each scenario challenges you to explore even the most basic assumptions surrounding your business.

Scenario-building is a proven way to test your organization's readiness to react to threats that are real and have a high probability of putting your organization under severe stress. In companies with massive long-term investments in fixed assets, like the oil and gas industry, scenarios are essential to developing plans for responding to various categories of crises beyond your control, for example, volatile prices, oil spills, tanker crashes, offshore platform disasters, international sanctions, or military actions.

Foresight practitioners commonly consider four trajectories for change when designing scenarios. At the University of Houston's foresight program, one of the preeminent foresight training programs in the world, Andy Hines built on the work of University of Hawaii futurist Jim Dator and identified four archetypes of change as guidelines for writing very distinct scenarios:

- *Baseline:* The gradual, linear, incremental change scenario. It's what happened yesterday and what you expect to happen tomorrow. This is often the kind of scenario planning we do in annual planning exercises in every organization because it's predictable.

- *New equilibrium:* Where we experience a new era because the domain is confronted with a major evolutionary challenge to how it's been operating and is forced to adapt and compromise to save itself, all while the basic structure of the system remains intact.

- *Collapse:* The worst-case scenario for your projected future. What if everything goes wrong and the system falls into dysfunction? The established way of doing things no longer works.

- *Transformation:* Where the domain has totally changed because of a big shift in technology, policy, or the economy. It's the hopeful opposite of the collapse scenario yet just as impactful. The rules of the game are scrapped, and new ones written.

For every signal that your team identifies as both high likelihood and high impact (quadrant 2 of the assessment matrix), the next step is to ask the relevant STEEP subgroup in your team to identify *how* that signal might impact key assumptions in your business. Specifically, ask this subgroup to identify what the future of your business would look like if these signals came true along the lines of the four archetypes: baseline, new equilibrium, collapse, and transformation. Turn each of these scenarios into a one-page action plan for what your organization would do if this scenario were to come true. And then ask your team's subgroups to present the scenarios at your quarterly team meeting, where you have more time to dedicate to foresight and planning than you do in just the thirty or forty minutes allotted at your monthly team meeting. Ask your subgroups to explore several questions: How do these scenarios affect your assessment of your organization's future? Do these scenarios create new pathways for exploration? Do they dispel assumptions? As a final step, give each scenario a simple, memorable name so they're more easily remembered and everyone on the team can easily understand what that signal and scenario plan mean. For example, one of the San Jose Sharks' scenarios for 2020 was called "No Fans in 2020," and everyone on the team knew exactly what that scenario represented. You won't know if any of these signals will actually come to fruition, but if they do, you will have developed a proactive action plan of what to do and how to respond.

For the San Jose Sharks, the result of its scenario plan was a rapid escalation in the organization's digital strategies. As a former top executive at SAP, Jonathan was a veteran of Silicon Valley and was accustomed to thinking in terms of transformational futures. He had been imploring his team to "think beyond the rink," but the reality of daily operations (the organization hosts more than 180 events per year) meant there was never time to plan to change. Through scenario planning, the whole organization found a way to operationalize making changes.

One of the team's scenarios had foreseen how badly the Sharks' loyal ticket holders would miss the live games and thirst for some way to stay engaged while at home. For many fans, attending games and concerts at the San Jose Sharks' stadium are *anchor moments* in their lives. They may not remember the actual event, but the pageantry and ritual of attending a live event is seared in fans' minds, which translates into a lifetime of loyalty. Without anchor moments to support their fan base, how would the Sharks support their long-term business model?

An ambitious plan evolved by streaming *simulated* Sharks' games on the popular video game and social media platform Twitch. The Sharks carried out bold experiments like allowing real-life fans to dress up virtually and simulate being one of the players in the simulated game. Fans would upload their photos, their height, whether they shot from the left or from the right, and even got their names digitally printed on a custom virtual jersey. To make the simulated games more engaging, the Sharks went even further and asked their real-life play-by-play announcer to announce the games over Twitch. They even extended their real-life corporate sponsorships into their virtual season.

In an early simulation, one of the fans was digitally injured. The injury meant the end of the simulated game for this fan, and he was sorely disappointed—that is, until he saw himself being carried off the virtual ice by one of his favorite team players. Shortly thereafter, and in real life, the general manager of the Sharks called the actual fan and wished him a speedy recovery from the virtual injury. Shocked beyond belief about the real phone call after a simulated game, the fan posted on his social media channels, "Today I was a San Jose Shark, taking the place of my favorite player. I can die a happy man. Definitely a highlight of 2020, and one I will not soon forget." After only a few simulated games on Twitch, the Sharks had topped six million digital impressions. Not bad for an organization that didn't even have a digital engagement channel just weeks earlier.

Scenario planning also has a positive effect on executive team culture. Former Shell executive Ted Newland, who was a scenario team leader in the 1980s, said after his retirement, "In hindsight, the greatest value of scenarios is that they created a culture where you could ask anyone a question, and the answer would need to be contextual. Answering 'Because I'm the boss' or 'Because the business case is positive' was out-of-bounds."[10] Scenario planning not only encourages future thinking in your team members but also encourages them to be more open-minded about the present.

Because scenario planning can be time- and resource-intensive, many companies save the practice for times of crisis, an approach that is bound to have only a limited impact and be simply reactive. Nevertheless, scenarios are very effective in proactively building team capacity for organizational change. Through scenario planning, team members expand their imaginations beyond the everyday and learn to see possibilities and capabilities for the organization that they would otherwise have no way of seeing. In effect, they learn to predict possible futures and strengthen the team's radical adaptability to succeed no matter what may come.

Foster a Culture of Continuous Learning

We started this chapter by describing how the discipline of foresight involves thinking about the future and identifying what you need to do today to succeed tomorrow. Through the practice of detection, assessment, and scenario planning, we can increase our team's radical adaptability and train our organizational muscle to learn, unlearn, relearn, and repeat. All these practices are critical to competing in a new world of work rife with uncertainty and variability. That's what foresight does—it teaches your leaders to expand your organizational mindset for what's possible, it makes you and your colleagues smarter and better informed about the future, and it compels you to proactively win the fight for risk intelligence as if your organization's life depends on it.

Simulation exercises go one step beyond scenario planning and turn hypothetical paper ideas into real "war games" that improve our risk management and enhance our capabilities, processes, and cultures when we need to respond to a sudden shift in the environment. Here's one example. In 2007, during a time of diplomatic stress between Russia and Estonia, Russian proxies launched a cyberattack against Estonia's government, banks, media outlets, and IT communication systems.[11] At the time, it was the most sophisticated coordinated cyberattack ever. Not long after, Estonia worked with other North Atlantic Treaty Organization (NATO) members to organize Locked Shields, which has since become the largest annual cyber-war-game exercise in the world. The exercise is held every spring, when more than one thousand cybersecurity experts from thirty countries descend on Estonia's capital, Tallinn, for three days of cyber-war-gaming.

In the Locked Shields exercise, experts from Estonia play the part of the attacking "red team," while all the other NATO members play the defensive "blue team," tasked with defending more than four thousand virtual IT systems against twenty-five hundred virtual cyberattacks. The annual exercise helps all participating NATO countries recognize vulnerabilities in their cyber defenses and bolsters leadership competency through simulating complex problem-solving and strategic decision-making during a real cyber war.[12]

In another simulation exercise in May 2018, the Johns Hopkins Center for Health Security conducted the Clade X exercise in Washington, D.C. In this simulation, members of Congress participated in a game involving a public health crisis with a fictitious respiratory virus. The outcome of the game should be of no surprise in a post-coronavirus world: infections spread rapidly because half the people who had the virus showed no symptoms, and travel bans were ineffective in stopping the spread. Hospitals were overwhelmed, medical supplies ran out, and leaders from state and federal levels kept giving conflicting advice to the public. The exercise was a perfect dry run for the actual coronavirus pandemic less than two years later, except there is little to no evidence that anyone paid attention to the Clade X report before our struggle with a real virus.

Simulations and war games can uncover your organization's vulnerabilities to specific threats and can reveal problems with decision-making and leadership alignment. Clade X was a successful exercise because it pointed out the deficiencies in the US health-care system. The failure lay in American political leaders' inability to address those deficiencies, before a real virus appeared two years later and paralyzed the economy.[13]

Every foresight process prompts leaders in some way to delve more deeply into their decision-making processes and choices, and that, says Wharton professor Adam Grant, is key to becoming a learning organization. "To build a learning culture," he writes, "we need to create a specific kind of accountability—one that leads people to think again about their decisions." Grant points out that results-oriented leaders can be so focused on short-term performance that they fail to learn—and this proclivity makes them less adaptable. Leaders in high-performance cultures can be resistant to experimentation because they're always looking for guarantees of success and because that's what they are incentivized to do. It's the opposite in learning organizations. "The goal in a learning culture," he says, "is to welcome these kinds of experiments, and make "rethinking" so familiar that it becomes routine and people don't hesitate to pitch new ideas."[14]

Unfortunately, foresight has a habit of being a cyclical corporate strategy and risk intelligence exercise. In a crisis, you may have all hands on deck with your team to explore and dig yourself out of the crisis. But when times return to normal, it's not unheard-of for companies to stop scenario planning, revert to old ways, and get lazy and complacent.

When the pandemic struck in the early spring of 2020, Leo Tilman had just completed a series of war-game simulation exercises as part of a strategic and contingency planning process for a major client in the middle of a large merger. What the client's executive team members learned about their own company, its processes, and themselves, came in very handy soon afterward, when the pandemic forced everyone to adapt to new contingencies and emergencies.

"We are going to be in an environment of disruption, change, and uncertainty for the rest of our careers, even though the nature of dislocations is going to be different each time," Leo said. "Now we're dealing with a pandemic, but next time we're going to be dealing with a geopolitical crisis or a financial crisis or a disruptive technology. We will continue to deal with disruptions of completely different types, origins, and magnitudes. We need the capacity as an organization to do this over and over again, to navigate disruption and change so that we can adapt." That's what foresight helps you do.

Over the previous four chapters, we've explored the leadership competencies necessary to make your *team* radically adaptable through a set of high-return practices, processes, systems, and behaviors, which if mastered and layered on top of each other, create a self-reinforcing loop that gives your team lasting competitive advantage for the future. Now, in the remainder of the book, we turn our attention to how you can apply this new team flow state to make your *organization* radically adaptable, through your business model, workforce, and purpose. Applied at both the team and the enterprise level, radical adaptability creates an infinite loop of transformation that will help you compete and win in the new world of work. To get there, let's dive into how you can leverage your new foresight skills to look into the future and design your ideal business model for ten years out.

GUIDING QUESTIONS
How to Compete in the New World of Work

Does our team spend sufficient energy thinking about the future on a monthly basis?

> Do we use foresight to "look around corners," or do we just react to day-to-day challenges? The pace of change is accelerating exponentially, and the most successful teams will be those that deploy foresight to identify future opportunities and deflect unexpected risk.

Does our team have a solid understanding of the early-warning signals that can disrupt us and a method for assessing priorities?

> Foresight starts with risk detection and assessment. Radically adaptable companies engage in a structured and continuous process to scan the horizon, identify a portfolio of risks across five STEEP vectors, and develop risk radars to guide the team in prioritizing different threats and opportunities.

Does our team have action plans in place for various possible future states?

> By developing fast sprint action plans, our team has the advantage of time when risks do suddenly unfold. As an added benefit, scenario planning helps foster a culture of exploration, curiosity, and future thinking for our entire team.

Future-Proof Your Business Model

I n January 2021, General Motors CEO Mary Barra shocked the global auto industry by announcing plans to phase out all fossil-fueled models by 2035 and make the transition to an electric-only fleet. She promised to spend $27 billion toward the goal "and to set an example of responsible leadership in a world that is faced with climate change."[1]

At the time of the announcement, the world's fourth-largest carmaker had only one electric vehicle on the market, the Chevrolet Bolt hatchback. Out of GM's total global sales of 6.8 million vehicles in 2020, the company sold only 20,754 Chevy Bolts.[2] But Barra's team at GM had been slowly moving toward the electric-vehicle future for more than a decade. The time had finally come to confront the question: What business are we really in? Are we in the internal combustion business? Or is that just part of our legacy and how we have helped people move in the past? If we're not in the internal combustion business, then we should not be wedded to fossil fuel consumption, and we ought to make the transition to a fully electric auto manufacturer, which is better for the environment and better for our common future.

"Our hope," Barra wrote afterward, "was to excite and inspire everyone with the promise of an all-electric future—with the thrill of vehicles powered by electric propulsion and supported by advanced electrical architecture—reimagining what it means to move people and goods, including when there is no driver."[3]

GM had made similar transitions in the past. Billy Durant, who founded General Motors in 1908, had made his first fortune as owner of America's leading horse-drawn carriage manufacturer. He had been dubious about the early horseless carriages, but he also knew that they represented the future of transportation. Durant bankrolled GM from the riches he had earned as a maker of his soon-to-be obsolete carriages, just as surely as GM is now investing billions earned from the sale of gas guzzlers to build GM's emission-free future. The company is in the business of transporting people and goods through software and electricity, and adjacencies that enable that movement seamlessly and sustainably with low emissions. That's the story of its second century.

As you consider your role as a radically adaptable leader, it's time to pause and ask yourself, "What business are we really in?" Consider approaching this question from a first principles perspective, and question your major assumptions about your business and your industry. Think of yourself as a toddler, consistently questioning every new experience. "But why?" It's possibly the most annoying repeated phrase that parents must respond to, but a child's healthy development depends on the child's constant questioning of its perceptions of the world. The same can be said about you and your business.

It has been more than sixty years since marketing guru Theodore Levitt pointed out in *Harvard Business Review* that railroad companies were failing because they had failed their customers. Gorged on profits from their monopoly routes, the railroad barons assumed they were in the railroad business and saw the rise of other forms of transportation

High-Return Practices for Competing in the New World of Work

1. Zoom out to envision your industry ten years ahead.
2. Identify technologies poised for exponential growth.
3. Zoom in through rapid agile experimentation.
4. Create communities of raving customers.

only as competition. Had the railroads instead understood their role as transportation service providers, they could have used their enormous profits to invest in cars, trucks, airlines, and related industries that reflected the evolving preferences of their customers. Instead, the railroad barons gradually lost their customers and then, one by one, their companies.[4]

So, what business are you really in? Do you define your business by the products and services you currently sell or by the benefits your customers value? Theodore Levitt was fond of saying that no one buys quarter-inch drills. Customers buy quarter-inch holes. You can make the best quarter-inch drill bit on the market, but you'll have no customers if they find better ways to make quarter-inch holes. That's why GM is no longer positioned as a maker of internal combustion automobiles but as a provider of electric mobility solutions that are valued by customers because they are effective for transportation and good for the planet.

Four Steps to the Future

In our Go Forward to Work (GFTW) interviews and focus groups with over two thousand executives, we heard repeatedly how the pandemic had forced many of these business leaders to rethink their long-held assumptions about their industries and, in some cases, completely reinvent the way they earned revenue. Some were able to reengineer their businesses and, within a year, made changes that might have taken ten years to accomplish otherwise. A 2020 survey by Dell Technologies suggested that 80 percent of businesses had changed their business models that year. Indeed, the coronavirus pandemic poured gasoline on the fire of digital transformation and accelerated many trends already underway, from the adoption of new technologies to the automation of many jobs.

From this research, we've identified certain common patterns of business model reinvention practiced by the most successful companies. We've developed a four-step methodology your team can use to question your current business model and advance it toward the future.

Engaging in this methodology is an effective way of leveraging much of the foresight work your team has done in the previous chapter. You want to accept your ten-year vision of your industry as your company's preferred future state and then start experimenting toward that vision. Each year, as your team engages the pertinent technologies most likely to make long-term disruptive impacts on your business and your industry, you will be positioning your company to intercept those technologies' exponential growth curves and rise with them. And as you win customers' trust, you should leverage that into building communities and networks around your offerings, so your super fans protect your evolving business model like a moat around a castle.

Zoom Out to Envision Your Industry Ten Years Ahead

Our friend John Hagel, the retired co-chairman of Deloitte's Center for the Edge, has long advocated a powerful approach to business model reinvention that he calls *zooming out* and *zooming in*. John recommends that you zoom out first by asking two key questions: What will our industry look like in ten years' time? And what kind of company do we need to become to succeed in that future?

Zoom-out exercises of this kind invite leaders to make leaps of imagination in which growth is nonsequential, orthogonal, and exponential—very different from traditional three-year growth planning projections expressed in terms that are sequential, linear, and geometric.

The simplest way to see the difference is to picture the short-term and long-term paths of most business careers. Changes happen to most people from year to year in fairly orderly sequences, but the shape of change over the decades is almost always unexpected and nonlinear. Keith had been chief marketing officer at Starwood Hotels and then took a position at Mike Milken's right hand as one of his holding company CEOs. Then Keith started a firm that offered growth coaching to sales and marketing teams while he was searching for his next role. But when a sudden opportunity emerged to write a book—which became a *New York Times* bestseller—his team-coaching business took off exponentially. At any point along the way, if a time traveler had been able to tell him what he'd be doing in ten years from that moment, he would have said, "Most definitely not!"

That's the magic, and the burden, that we're presented by the opportunities and uncertainties of the future. It's precisely how the zoom-out process encourages executives to think about their businesses. Using the foresight tools of detection, assessment, and scenario planning, zooming out ten years allows your team to make meaning of the signals on your risk radar. Try using the collaborative problem-solving (CPS) process described in chapter 2 by putting the two critical zoom-out questions on the table: What does the ten-year future of our industry look like? And what is our desired position in that future? If you've already developed some scenarios for five years out, use CPS to debate how they might play out for another five years. The answers you come up with might include the need for previously unexpected capabilities, markets, products, resources, and behaviors.

This kind of zoom-out exercise can be done at your team's annual strategic planning meeting. But it is most decidedly not a solitary exercise or limited to just your team, and you should involve anyone who can help you encapsulate that vision. You may find it useful to consult with specialists in certain technical areas to help your team think through various scenarios involving your industry's long-term trajectory. Consider the vital role of inclusion and teaming out, so that everyone in your company's expanded vision of a team is involved and committed to the agreed-on next steps. Ultimately, the goal of this zoom-out exercise is to develop a shared long-term team vision and a road map for making decisions along the way.

Identify Technologies Poised for Exponential Growth

Zooming out forces you to speculate about the next ten years of technological progress and how those technologies might remake your industry several times over in that time span. Next, you want to explore those emerging technologies and envision the opportunities to grow along with them. Technological growth by its nature follows an exponential growth curve, and your company can enjoy a similar pace of growth if you are able to engage with the right technologies early on.

Domino's Pizza emerged as one of the business world's unlikely winners during the 2020 pandemic year, largely because of its advanced commitment to technology. As the largest pizza company in the world as measured by sales, Domino's had spent several years prior to the pandemic building up its digital transformation efforts and developing unique capabilities in touchless transactions and omnichannel e-commerce functionality—all of which proved incredibly useful during the pandemic. In a year when thousands of eat-in restaurants permanently closed, takeout providers managed to survive. Domino's, however, outstripped all its competitors in the takeout pizza sector, with a 16 percent increase in demand over the previous year and a 30 percent increase in net profit.[5] How was it able to do so?

One key reason for Domino's success was its constant pursuit of innovation in its delivery channel. Unlike its pizza competitors who use third-party delivery companies like DoorDash and Grubhub, Domino's made a strategic decision to only use its own delivery fleet so that it could capture that most precious resource of every forward-thinking business: customer data. "We've got a tremendous customer base and data set," said Domino's CEO Ritch Allison of his eighty-five million customers. I just cannot imagine why we would want to give that to a competitor." About DoorDash, Grubhub, and the others, he added "Let's be clear, these aggregators are ultimately competitors of the restaurant companies they serve."[6]

DoorDash and the other third-party food delivery companies make it easier for competing pizza chains to reach more customers and scale up during surges in demand. But the average 30 percent commission they take off the total sale eats into pizza chains' profit margins. To maintain its own delivery fleet, Domino's, on the other hand, must constantly recruit drivers, which is especially difficult in tight job markets. That problem, however, led Domino's to seek a technology solution: making deliveries through autonomous robotic vehicles. Starting in 2016, the company ran four pilot experiments to test different delivery robot systems and to learn how to overcome operational hurdles and deliver customer satisfaction. Until the pandemic put a temporary halt to the project, Domino's was prepared to unveil a robotic delivery partnership with Nuro, a robotics company based in Houston.[7] Robotic delivery remains a key part of Domino's zoom-out future, nonetheless. By 2024, the autonomous robotic delivery market is expected to be worth $34 billion—almost three times what it was in 2018.[8] Domino's strategic decision to jump on the rapidly accelerating growth of autonomous robotic delivery will help the company take a slice out of the huge future market for autonomous fast-food delivery.

One lesson of Domino's experience is that while competitors give away their data to third-party delivery services, Domino's has used its captured customer data and its proprietary delivery system to intercept the exponential growth curve of advancing technologies. Investors have rewarded the vision, and by the end of 2020, Domino's stock price had doubled from three years earlier, helping provide the capital the company will need to advance faster and farther toward its zoom-out vision.

The value of adopting exponential technology as a business transformation tool applies to all industries. Consider the case of American energy company NOV, which manufactures heavy equipment for the oil, gas, and renewable energy industries. Its equipment is required to work in complex, rugged, and extreme environments like deep under water, the North Pole region, and distant deserts. But most of these places make access to equipment data difficult, if not impossible. Providing cloud connectivity is an option in some places but is still limited.

To complicate matters further, energy operations often involve numerous service providers, with equipment from multiple manufacturers that create unique data streams that don't readily interface with other systems. For example, a single oil well site can have roughly three hundred different data sources contributing to the drilling production, and all have different communication protocols and control systems.

So over the last few years, NOV started building smart functionality into all its equipment so that it can analyze and compute data remotely on-site, where all the activity happens in the field. Long-term, NOV imagines a zoom-out future where automation and self-driving are the norm in the energy sector. But to get there, the industry needs to harness the potential of exponential technologies like industrial Internet of Things (IoT) so machines can communicate seamlessly with each other remotely.

At *Fortune* 500 powerhouse NOV, these efforts have resulted in a technical solution called Max Edge, which connects local control systems and machinery and enables NOV to collect high-speed data, analyze and interact with it in real time, and provide on-the-ground advisory to control systems, even if there's limited internet access. This capability greatly simplifies machine communications and automation across the ecosystem. During the early days of the pandemic, it also came in handy when onsite staff availability was limited. NOV could rely on Max Edge technology to monitor field operations remotely, since the company's equipment was essential to keep the world economy flowing.

As the pandemic continued, David Reid, NOV's chief marketing officer and chief technology officer, sensed an opportunity to leverage Max Edge and create a potential new revenue stream outside NOV's traditional manufacturing business model: one that involved data, software delivery, and connectivity through a "platform as a service."

"In this new world," David said, "we're not just offering a physical product, which is our core, but we're also able to offer a new digital service based on Max Edge capability." The pandemic propelled NOV to leverage its existing IoT technology, create new software services for its hardware clients, and accelerate the industry's move toward automation. "With this new data delivery platform, we're increasingly becoming both a software and hardware company."

Beyond large *Fortune* 1000 enterprises like Domino's Pizza and NOV, consider how smaller organizations in different industries have also incorporated new technologies to evolve their businesses. Founded in 1985 by Ivan Misner, BNI is a business referral network for executives, entrepreneurs, and small-business owners. The network has more than ten thousand chapters and more than 280,000 members worldwide. Every week, BNI chapters meet to conduct a standardized networking program focused on targeted referrals. Members stand up and have thirty to sixty seconds to introduce themselves and their work. After self-introductions, members stand up again and individually offer specific referrals in their personal networks that might be potential clients for other chapter members.

These aren't just casual referrals. BNI members develop deep social capital with each other and believe that both parties benefit when they refer their personal social networks to other BNI members. They call this core value *givers gain*. And indeed, in 2020 BNI passed 11.5 million referrals to their members, generating more than $16 billion worth of business for members. That's more than twice the GDP of the country of Lichtenstein!

In 2018, Ivan suggested to the company's board of directors that the future of face-to-face networking is *online* and that unless BNI experimented with and adopted new technologies like mixed reality, holographic presence, and video communication channels, BNI would be negatively disrupted in its next decade. He was prescient and foresaw the rise of remote work, even before the pandemic. By March 2020, all ten thousand BNI chapters had pivoted to online networking—a dramatic business shift for an organization with a three-decade history dedicated to in-person business networking. Fast-forward to mid-2021, and BNI *added* five hundred new chapters during the pandemic year, all of which have only ever met online! Such growth thus confirms Ivan's belief that every organization needs to adopt new technologies, or be disrupted.

How should you think about which technologies to include in your zoom-out vision? Keith and Kian's friend Peter Diamandis—founder and chairman of the XPRIZE Foundation—has studied countless industries where he has recognized a clear-cut pattern in the growth of digital technologies and their interaction with business, which Peter calls the *six Ds*. As domains adopt digital technology and informational properties, they *digitize* into bits and bytes and jump on the curve of exponential change as described by Moore's law, which observes how computational price and performance ratios double exponentially every eighteen to twenty-four months. The problem is that the early doublings are *deceptive* and easy to miss because they are so small (e.g., 1, 2, 4, 8, 16, 32 . . .), but it takes only a few exponential steps for the technology to pop and *disrupt* markets for everyone who wasn't cognizant of the technology early on. Most businesses make the mistake of failing to see the early benefits of new technology and then get overwhelmed by its sudden exponential growth.

One of the primary effects of exponential technology on business is that it digitizes the functions of material objects so the objects are no longer needed. The functions become *dematerialized*. The smartphone, for example, has digitized the functions of a number of material objects—typewriters, cameras, music players, video recorders, and books, newspapers, and magazines. This dematerialization leads to a drop in prices as every new unit's marginal cost approaches zero and the product in turn becomes *demonetized.*

At first, demonetization is disruptive to industries when it leads to lower total revenues. But if you can identify which two or three exponential technologies are potentially the most disruptive for your industry, you can benefit because demonetarization ultimately leads to a much larger mass market when the domain explodes. At that point, the technology is *democratized* and you can scale globally.

Which technologies should you pay attention to? Surely, you have heard of some of these transformative technologies. Our goal here isn't to provide a comprehensive analysis of all the technologies to look out for but rather to highlight a few domains that are growing exponentially and that will be massively disruptive to all businesses over the next decade. Your fiduciary responsibility, and your opportunity, as a leader is to identify which two or three exponential technologies are potentially the most disruptive for your industry and intercept these exponential change curves to ultimately benefit from this technological disruption and to future-proof your business model for the decade ahead.

AI as a service

Peter Diamandis likes to say that there will be two types of companies in ten years' time: "AI-led companies, and dead companies." We want to make sure you fall into the former camp, not the latter. Every company must, at the very minimum, develop a strong AI competency in addition to any other exponential technologies relevant for its industry. Peter, for example, is disrupting his own business of providing exponential technology education by building an AI that can help him search the web for evidence of abundance and longevity. He has built a machine learning algorithm called Futureloop, which scours thousands of online news sources daily, identifies the most relevant highlights of abundance, and then packages it as a daily email for his clients. Now, you don't need to build your own AI capability like Peter has done; you can "borrow" or "rent" this capability using software-as-a-service AI platforms.

Well before 2030, we will see the emergence of powerful cloud tools known as AI as a service (AIaaS)—which will allow every business leader to incorporate AI into different functional domains. AIaaS will collaborate with employees in everyday business operations, including helping with rote tasks, more creative idea generation, accounting and finance, customer service, business intelligence, and HR. These AIaaS tools will allow companies of all sizes to rent the world's most powerful computing tools and apply them to existing data. For example, the new Amazon Personalize machine learning platform enables clients to engage the power of Amazon's machine learning capabilities to create individualized recommendations for their consumers, using that company's proprietary data.

AIaaS will be propelled by the increasing ubiquity of cloud computing and—software as a service (SaaS). Cisco estimates that 70 percent of all enterprise workflow in 2021 is happening in the cloud, using SaaS enterprise platforms. AI has already begun to integrate into many of these SaaS platforms, from recommendation engines on GitHub to real-time grammar recommendations using Grammarly. In fact, what we call AIaaS now seems destined to become just a part of standard operating procedure. Mark Weiser, the onetime chief technology officer of Xerox PARC, has often been quoted as saying, "The most profound technologies are those that disappear. They weave themselves into the fabric of everyday things until they become indistinguishable." That's the future of AIaaS.

Quantum computing

The next era of computing will be propelled by quantum computing, which will radically change the nature of a wide range of industries, including finance, materials science, logistics, supply chain, biotechnology, and computer network security itself. Right now, some problems we face are too complex to solve or predict because they have seemingly infinite variables. But quantum computers can simultaneously process a vastly larger range of values than even the most powerful of today's supercomputers. That means quantum computers will be capable of quickly solving many problems that are currently too complex because of their vast numbers of variables. Quantum computing can optimize systems like supply chains and logistics and create breakthroughs in materials design, chemistry, and pharmaceuticals. Quantum computing would likely have arrived at the formula for a coronavirus vaccine even faster than it was developed.

How do quantum computers work? In classical computing, everything is digitized into either a 0 or a 1 in software bits. You're either one, or the other. But in quantum computing, quantum bits (known as *qubits*) can exist simultaneously as both 0s and 1s, in a phenomenon known as *quantum superposition*. The practical implication is that qubits can consider multiple simultaneous outcomes in a single calculation. So 1 qubit can consider 2 outcomes, or 2 calculations, 2 qubits can do 4 calculations, 3 qubits can do 8, and 4 qubits can do 16. You can, hopefully, see the exponential pattern here. By the time you have 30 qubits on a computer chip, your quantum computer can do 1 billion calculations! By 300 qubits, quantum computers will be able to do more calculations than there are atoms in the universe.

Today's quantum computers have limited practical applications because they are huge and require precise lab environments to function. In the next five years, however, quantum computing will be available as a cloud service provided by all the competing tech giants—Google, Amazon, Microsoft, IBM, and others.

Avatar systems

Since 2016, we've seen the emergence of new user interfaces like augmented reality and virtual reality open new pathways for humans to experience education, entertainment, and empathy, via remote connectivity.

These user interfaces change the linear narrative of how we do things: we no longer have to go somewhere—as we humans have evolved to do—to experience things. And the pandemic poured fuel on the need to experience things remotely.

In 2018, the XPRIZE Foundation launched a $10 million competition to develop a physical, nonautonomous avatar system with which an operator can see, hear, and interact within a remote environment in a manner that feels as if they are truly there. By 2030, these avatars could provide the experience of your presence regardless of your location, allowing you to "jack-in" to an avatar located anywhere on earth. Health-care professionals could provide medical care in disaster zones and other remote locations, skilled technicians could respond more quickly to the need for expertise, and research and exploration work could take place where humans can't go. Visiting via avatar could replace some forms of travel and tourism. Instead of videoconferencing via Zoom as we did to get through the pandemic, we'll instead "rem-in" (remote-in) virtually. By 2030, our limitations of time and space will radically shift, and countless business opportunities will open up as these and other user interfaces make possible a whole new realm of remote interactions.

Blockchain

Digital assets like Bitcoin and other cryptocurrencies are growing in appeal because they are based on blockchain technology, a distributed database of encrypted information that is stored in duplicate on hundreds of thousands of computers worldwide. Blockchain databases can store all kinds of information, like digital identities and provenance, and even provide the ability to own and trade digital assets (like digital art) through peer-to-peer channels via non-fungible tokens. Because the users of the network collectively control it, blockchain technology offers a new pathway to verify trust. If your business relies on trust and verification in any way, blockchain technologies can help you build a radically different business model in the future. Analysis by PwC in 2020 suggested that blockchain technology could boost the global gross domestic product by $1.76 trillion in the following decade, with the greatest impact being on tracking supply-chain products and services, followed by payments and financial services, and identity management to help curb fraud and identity theft. In fact, blockchain technology will introduce a new era on the internet, what some call Web 3.0, where all transactions are made directly on a peer-to-peer basis, posing a direct disruptive threat to all the businesses we currently rely on as intermediary brokers of trust.

The spatial web

The pandemic supercharged the desire to connect in virtual environments beyond videoconferencing, and now entrepreneurs are building the next era of the spatial web, where individuals will interact with each other not through screens but within three-dimensional spaces combining both real and virtual locations. What the World Wide Web did for connecting websites, the spatial web will do for connecting people, physical spaces, and digital assets. To get to that next level of seamless integration within our lives, we will need to see widespread 5G connectivity and mass adoption of smart glasses and other augmented-reality devices, both of which we expect to occur by the mid-2020s. But the practical manifestation of the spatial web is already here through the convergence of blockchain-based digital objects, phone-based augmented reality, web-enabled virtual reality, head-mounted displays, spatial sound and audio, and unique gamification techniques.

The spatial web will bring new opportunities for collaboration and new service models for many businesses. Eric Pulier, founder and CEO of the similarly named company Spatial Web, said, "Spatial web ventures are already making inroads into how we meet, shop, engage with marketing experiences, and interact with one another. And it's just the beginning." For example, if your customers can't attend a physical venue or retail location, you could mail them a virtual-reality or an augmented-reality headset so the person could "visit" the showroom without leaving home. Through these headsets, your client can hear spatial audio and see physical products remotely. Instead of attending conferences in person, companies can hold events in the spatial web, where attendees can interact virtually through digital avatars and with many more attendees possible than a typical physical event.

In short, when AIaaS converges with 5G, billions of connected devices, blockchain technologies, and new user interfaces like augmented reality and robotic avatars, we will see an exponential growth in dematerialized companies over the next decade. These firms will be unencumbered by physical space or hardware infrastructure and will be able to scale worldwide with remotely hosted operations and teams. As you consider which exponential technologies to integrate with your zoom-out vision, remember that some of these technologies will have different timelines for commercialization and maturation. For all of these technologies, there will be no specific moment in the future when it will be suddenly "ready" and will take over the way we live and work. The pieces that collectively make up the spatial web, for instance, are each on their own exponential growth curves, in which each is becoming increasingly more useful and powerful. The key here is that you need to experiment with these exponential technologies *now*; otherwise, you'll miss intercepting these growth curves and will be behind your competition when these technologies suddenly pop and become mainstream in the future.

Zoom In through Rapid Agile Experimentation

To zoom in on the future and leverage one or two technologies that give you the greatest chance of catching a wave of exponential growth, John Hagel suggests identifying two high-impact experimental projects that can be completed within the next six to twelve months and would move your company in the direction of your zoom-out vision.

This short-term goal requires an agile approach in proof of concept, experimentation, iteration, and deployment, and it's just short enough to not get bogged down in two- or three-year plans.

At Ferrazzi Greenlight, where our zoom-out vision foresees team coaching fully powered by AI, we launched a short-term zoom-in project that incorporates currently available algorithmic assessments into one of our existing team diagnostic tools. Implementing this modest, imperfect project is teaching us a lot about what it will take to achieve our zoom-out vision. At drone startup Birdstop, where the zoom-out vision is to generate on-demand aerial imaging through a cloud-based network of autonomous drones, the interim zoom-in project looks like this: colocate drone stations in high-demand zones to test whether corporate clients would be open to sharing the drone network rather than having a network solely for their own infrastructure observation. If the zoom-in experiment is successful, then over time, these local colocated networks could be connected to a larger mesh to provide continuous on-demand cloud observations.

One benefit of zooming in is that it allows your team to make small, strategic, high-impact annual bets about the future without committing to long-term, multiyear projects. If the exercise proves fruitful at the end of a quarterly or six-month sprint, resources could be added to accelerate the project's impact. If the experiment doesn't result in hopeful ways or no longer aligns with your annual zoom-out vision, you can pivot to new zoom-in projects. Along the way, you will constantly learn what works after every zoom-in project, and this will help cultivate a learning mindset within your leadership culture.

Over time, these zoom-in experiments, no matter how small, can snowball and develop into more ambitious projects that can transform the company on a trajectory toward your ten-year zoom-out vision. When designing your zoom-in experiment, pay special attention to who you task to join the project. You will want a mix of both domain experts and passionate team members from your existing team; these two groups can collaborate to solve problems creatively and push through obstacles. Your zoom-in team should report directly to you as the leader, and not in a matrix, so that it has the maximum permission possible to try new things and break existing dependencies on established internal processes like IT, marketing, and HR. You want this zoom-in team to have as much flexibility as possible to achieve its goal.

Consider how Ognomy, a mobile app for sleep apnea diagnosis, was developed as a zoom-in project by Dr. Dan Rifkin, a neurologist in Buffalo, New York. Sleep apnea is a potentially lethal sleep-related breathing disorder that impacts a billion people worldwide and goes mostly undiagnosed. By some estimates, 80 percent of people with apnea in the United States never get a diagnosis because of the expense and inconvenience of having to spend nights being monitored at specialized sleep clinics.[9]

Ognomy's trajectory exploded during the pandemic, when medical sleep clinics were forced to shut down. Patients were desperate for treatment, and a virtual diagnostics platform became more critical than ever before. The app allows patients to meet with doctors virtually and get tested, diagnosed, and treated from the comfort of their homes. Ognomy now serves doctors in sleep specialties as a transformative "practice in a box."

Dan Rifkin came to believe in the late 2010s that telemedicine and other digital tools could make diagnosis and treatment for sleep apnea more accessible and affordable. When he zoomed out ten years, he foresaw a platform that democratized access to sleep apnea diagnoses, so that millions who suffer from the condition could get tested and treated even if they didn't live near a physical sleep lab.

Over the years, Dan experimented with several videoconferencing platforms and different electronic medical record solutions to build his zoom-out vision. He found them all lacking and became convinced that to transform the treatment of sleep apnea, he had to create a stand-alone software solution that digitized every step of diagnosis, and treatment in the workflow of his practice. In June 2019, he led a two-day design workshop at Buffalo Niagara Medical Campus, where a team of twelve drew up a digital version of an at-home sleep apnea testing and treatment experience, with the goal of building an app within six months.

Over the two days, Dan's team took apart each step of his medical work-flow: initial examination, ordering sleep studies, diagnosing results, and managing patient records. The team also captured the user experience for patients, clinicians, and health-care administrators in a story-board that could inform the app design. Finally, they developed a virtual assistant chatbot to guide patients through the new app.

When the pandemic hit in March 2020, Dan had just hired the software development firm TopCoder to build the Ognomy app, with a target date of June 2020 for a minimum viable product (MVP). Suddenly, Dan was forced to close all seven of his sleep apnea labs, and so he pushed the TopCoder software team to deliver the Ognomy MVP within thirty days. To meet this ambitious deadline, thousands of developers from all over the world crowdsourced the software development and together created a user-friendly app that was ready to be tested and deployed by late April 2020.

"I realized very quickly," Dan said, "that we didn't need physical space anymore to practice sleep apnea diagnosis. Starting a digital practice definitely cannibalized my own practice in the short term, but Ognomy convinced me that I can do the work entirely digitally. Once I saw the power of the app, I began to pivot and digitize my entire practice." In early 2020, he thought it would take three to four years for both patients and doctors to get comfortable with telemedicine treatment of apnea. "Covid," he said, "supercharged that adoption overnight."

Fast-forward to 2021, and more than two thousand patients are registered on Ognomy, with new doctors joining the platform through a monthly subscription fee and pay-per-patient usage model. Dan believes that apps like Ognomy will change the face of access for sleep patients and the way sleep apnea is diagnosed and treated, just as he had predicted with his zoom-out vision a few years ago. Going forward, sleep labs will only be used for more complicated sleep studies, like narcolepsy or other sleep disorders.

"Five years from now, I will definitely still see some patients in the clinic, in order to maintain direct patient contact," he said. "But I believe a large part of my practice will transition to being the CEO of Ognomy."

Dan did a number of things right, which is how his one-year zoom-in experiment ended up transforming his business and may well transform his entire medical field. First and foremost, he designed his MVP so that it could scale rapidly. His efforts at digitizing his business show that in order to reach a billion people with your product or service, you have to radically rethink your delivery model. In the past, patients had to live near an urban area or a sleep center to get great care. That's no longer the case, because of Ognomy. "We've democratized access to sleep apnea diagnosis and treatment worldwide," Dan said, "and our market is the world, not just Buffalo, New York."

Second, he worked with a diverse team to get the best results. In his initial design workshop, his team of twelve had a wide variety of skill sets that complemented each other well and would reflect the great diversity of patients and caregivers who would eventually be using the app. This last point is important for people doing zoom-in projects in large organizations. It's critical that the team be staffed for passion first, and then skills. Zoom-in projects can often hit roadblocks, so you want a team that is passionate about solving problems creatively and that won't give up just because it encounters problems.

In this agile journey, you may feel like some of your zoom-in efforts are disappointing or that the technology is not as mature as you had hoped. But don't be fooled. You need to remember how exponential technologies grow slowly before they explode. The key here is to continue experimenting with agile zoom-in projects to get closer to your zoom-out vision. Some experiments will prove more fruitful than others, but your organization will benefit nevertheless through a culture of learning and experimentation.

Create Communities of Raving Customers

Given how exponential technology has the power to transform industries overnight, we believe it's also critical to go beyond mere product, service, and technology innovation—all of which can be replicated or disrupted—and foster communities to complement the technology, to help you withstand copycatting, and to make your business more resilient in times of uncertainty.

The innovation strategist Larry Keeley, in his seminal work *Ten Types of Innovation*, outlined how the most successful companies—as measured by stock price on the S&P 500—integrated multiple innovation types into their business, from product innovation, channel innovation, service innovation, to process innovation.[10] As we enter a new era where new technologies like AI and blockchain will democratize and decentralize access to many products and services, we believe it's critical to innovate your network channel, foster your community, and build it into a defensible moat. A moat can help strengthen your resiliency to pivot and navigate in rough seas. And it can differentiate you when networks and platforms decentralize.

When college campuses closed down because of the pandemic in the spring of 2020, the crisis delivered a harsh body blow to an upstart national nonprofit called Swipe Out Hunger. Led by founder and CEO Rachel Sumekh, Swipe Out Hunger is dedicated to eradicating food insecurity on college campuses, where one in three students faces hunger. With programs located on more than 140 college campuses, one of the nonprofit's programs is called the Swipe Drive, which enables students to donate their extra cafeteria meal-plan dollars to their peers facing food insecurity on campus.

Swipe Out Hunger had been growing fast when the pandemic shut down a major distribution channel and program model. Student food insecurity still existed, so Rachel and her team made a pivot to meet the moment. They leaned into Swipe Out Hunger's community of activists to innovate a new business model tailored to the pandemic. With board approval, they launched a new program called the Student Navigator Network, which hired college students from Swipe Out Hunger's network across the country and trained them to support their peers in finding food resources in their communities. Over two months, these ambassadors helped more than seven thousand college students gain access to $900,000 worth of food and other financial benefits so that these students could continue their studies throughout the pandemic.

"We went from a campus-based program to leaning into our community and asking them to help us develop a nationwide program where geography didn't matter," said Rachel. To get there, she hosted weekly virtual webinars, convening students, grassroots staff, and food policy experts so they could jointly ideate, test, iterate, and roll out the new model. Rachel said, "Administrators—which serve as our program's gatekeepers on campus—always think they know best, but in this case, we needed to bypass them as intermediaries and communicate directly with students on the ground to connect them to each other and leverage best practices from one campus to another." The pivot was so successful that Swipe Out Hunger expanded to twenty new college campuses during the pandemic. And it received a large grant to build a citywide hunger eradication program for college students in New York City. In addition, Swipe Out Hunger helped to pass legislation in numerous states to address food insecurity for college students.

"As the pandemic recedes and college campuses open up again, we'll have some space to consider what strategic choices we make," said Rachel. "We're now no longer just a one rocket ship; we're like a gardener with multiple flower beds, which can grow to feed a much larger community. We wouldn't have been able to pivot without leveraging our existing network of passionate student advocates, who helped us ideate and iterate our future."

The clear lesson from Swipe Out Hunger is to lean into your community in uncertain times. Crises are often community-building opportunities that can leave your organization stronger if you pay them proper attention.

Colin Sprake, an entrepreneur who owns a consulting firm called Make Your Mark, had a similar experience with his community. He helps couple-owned small businesses live more consciously and has more than 110,000 business owners in his community in Canada. In the early days of the lockdown, he started hosting a daily free one-hour call-in podcast for ten weeks. There, he would invite some of the most compelling thought leaders in business to join the calls and teach his community, for free, all in service to help his community manage through the daily challenges of the pandemic. The calls were so popular that at one point, more than three thousand community members would join Colin's daily calls. When the pandemic forced Colin to shut down his own live events-training business, Colin went to his community and asked for help on how to pivot, and literally thousands of his community members responded with advice, because they wanted to give back to Colin and help him through his business challenges. By the end of 2020, Colin's business had the best year ever, and his community membership grew by 100 percent from before the pandemic. "In the twenty-first century," he said, "if you're not building a community as part of your business, you're doing it wrong."

The ability of small organizations like these to thrive under such adverse conditions points to the increasing phenomenon of digital democratization and the transfer of power and decision-making from a central gatekeeper authority—governments, traditional media, financial markets, and so forth—to peer-to-peer networks of tech-enabled individuals.

In an increasingly decentralized world where technology democratizes access to anything and everything, power lies within communities of individuals who can radically disrupt the status quo. In this decade, what will differentiate you from your competitors will be how you foster, nurture, and harness your community and build a defensible moat against the competition.

In late January 2021, a crowd of retail investors on the microblogging service Reddit helped drive the price of a few stocks to astronomical heights and had financial markets reeling. It started when individual investors on Wall Street Bets, a Reddit subgroup, began buying the stock of a few companies that some financial analysts and hedge funds had bet against, including video game retailer GameStop. In a seven-day span, GameStop's price increased 600 percent, while institutional investors caught in a short squeeze against GameStop ultimately lost $70 billion in value. This episode led to several brokerage firms, including most famously Robinhood, to cease the trading of a few viral stocks, including GameStop. This pause outraged many small retail investors, who accused brokerage firms like Robinhood of protecting entrenched financial institutions over retail investors. "Robinhood or Robbing the 'Hood'?" tweeted one longtime fan of the company. What started as an internet chat room meme quickly escalated into a David versus Goliath story, all made possible by the cumulative power of individual actors (in this case, Reddit readers of the subreddit r/wallstreetbets) who rallied as a community to take down the Goliaths of the financial industry.

The GameStop short squeeze is unlikely to be a one-time blip in financial history. We're now witnessing a grand experiment in the decentralization of finance (known colloquially as *DeFi*), where groups of empowered individuals will just bypass established gatekeeper financial institutions and transact directly using blockchain technologies and peer-to-peer networks. Now imagine how circumstances may have turned out differently if Robinhood had instead cultivated the community of small retail investors and asked for their help rather than try to stop their trading. The brokerage would have had an army of fans, not a riotous financial mob.

The forces of democratization were also behind the rise of Clubhouse, which distinguished itself in February 2021 as the fastest startup in history to reach the "unicorn" valuation of $1 billion.[11] The founders of Clubhouse created a decentralized audio broadcasting social network allowing anyone from around the world to join conversation chat rooms and communicate to millions of people in real time using audio, without any barriers.

Clubhouse's new social network disrupted existing social networks by shifting conversations away from one-to-many asynchronous broadcasts found elsewhere on social media to decentralized many-to-many synchronous conversations. By recognizing the desire of people to find community online in a much more authentic way than any other social media network to date, Clubhouse started taking audience away from other streaming services like Spotify and YouTube.

The same disruptive democratizing effects can be seen in traditional media, where superstar journalists are leaving traditional news outlets and launching self-published, paid membership newsletters. By doing so, they remove the intermediary institution—in this case, the editor and publisher—and create a community of consumers interested in their work. For example, the political commentator Andrew Sullivan left *New York* magazine to self-publish a weekly subscription newsletter on the platform Substack and has almost instantly increased his income many-fold by creating a community of fans willing to pay to be part of his ecosystem.

These examples show how empowered communities win in decentralized systems by radically altering how value is captured: where, when, and by whom. If you think your business is safe from the forces of decentralization, think again. It's critical to foster a community of fans who can help your organization withstand the tides of uncertainty and propel you to new chapters, even as technology evolves and disrupts your competition.

James DeJulio, cofounder and CEO of crowd-driven advertising firm Tongal said, "Community is everything for your business. If you do it right, your community can market for you, they can innovate for you, and they can give you feedback. Why wouldn't you want that extra layer of power and support?"

The lesson is clear from our research: a community of devoted fans, if their purpose and passion is leveraged for good, can come to your rescue when you're most in need. So it's time to ask yourself, Who are my company's superfans? And who would come to our aid when seas are rough? Build a moat around your business model, and the power of the communities you attract can help your organization stay resilient in times of distress. In the final two chapters, we'll show how reinventing your business model can help you redesign your workforce and lead with your foremost values in mind to separate your organization from all the rest, and *win* in this new world of work.

GUIDING QUESTIONS
How to Compete in the New World of Work

Does our company actively envision what our industry will look like in a decade?

> Radically adaptable companies actively engage the collective brain trust of their senior leaders, board members, advisers, and staff members to zoom out using foresight tools and imagine the industry landscape a decade out.

How does our company incorporate frontier technologies?

> Do we take consistent, strategic, and potentially high-impact short-term zoom-in bets using new technologies to move the company toward our long-term zoom-out vision? These bets are structured as short-horizon, experimental projects that are free from traditional bureaucracy and often challenge the status quo thinking in the company.

How do we build community around every aspect of our company?

> Decentralized systems are changing the dynamics of power within industries, so the most radically adaptable companies leverage communities of consumers and fans to build moats around existing business models to withstand future uncertainty and commodification.

Build a Lego Block Workforce

Mariya Filipova hung up the phone, took off her signature bright-red eyeglasses, and sat down to consider what to do next. It was the beginning of the pandemic. Her boss had just asked her to reduce her department's operating expenses and rethink her staffing model in a way that did not impact the service they provided to their customers. She was to report back with a process that could be replicated elsewhere in the company. In these early days of the pandemic, everyone was managing cash outlays carefully, and Mariya's employer was no different. Because Mariya had a reputation for finding creative solutions, her team was tasked to take on this project and provide a playbook for the rest of the organization. She had until the end of the day to call her boss back with a proposed plan.

As the vice president of innovation at an insurance giant that manages health benefits for more than forty million Americans, Mariya was responsible for driving innovation, changing internal behaviors, and incubating new technology solutions that would improve patients' lives.[1] She managed a team of more than forty people within a much larger organization of seventy thousand–plus employees. Reducing her operations budget meant figuring out how to do more, with fewer resources.

She needed to find a way to not only maintain the work they had planned for 2020 but also accelerate their project timelines, given the urgency of the coronavirus pandemic. Mariya knew that *now*, more than ever, patients needed the solutions her team was developing, to help them navigate the stress and uncertainty this pandemic had put on them and their families.

The situation brought her back to the time when she herself was a patient at Massachusetts General Hospital in Boston three years earlier. She had just been diagnosed with a football-sized kidney tumor. "Mariya, we're sorry," her doctors told her. "There's no playbook for dealing with something like this, it's unprecedented," their words came back, as the bitterness of uncertainty sunk in.

Three years later, Mariya found herself in another unprecedented situation with no playbook to follow in the middle of a pandemic. She drew strength from her personal journey and set out to make her team better prepared for the future. To do that, Mariya had to go back to the core of what her team did best. She thought of the "jobs" that had to be done and the outcomes that needed to be accomplished. Reconstructing the team members' workflow into jobs to be done was going to be key to redesigning a workforce that was efficient, agile, and resilient.

With renewed energy, Mariya saw her plan come together: she had to make some key decisions about her workforce and how to work remotely, crowdsource, outsource, and augment the team with technology. She was now ready to call her boss back with the beginnings of a silver-lining playbook.

As we followed Mariya's journey and that of many other executives who were redesigning their workforce in the midst of a global pan-

---

High-Return Practices for Competing in the New World of Work

1. Ask, "What work needs to be done?"
2. Ask, "What workforce will we engage?"
3. Ask, "Where will the workforce work?"
4. Execute the transition.

---

demic, we gleaned insights on their decisions that helped them become radically adaptable in unprecedented times. This chapter is their playbook for how to build the workforce of the future.

The Lego Block Workforce

Every parent's worst nightmare is waking up at 3 a.m., walking across the bedroom in the dark, and stepping barefoot on that spiky Lego block left surreptitiously like a land mine by an enemy toddler. We all know these interlocking multicolored plastic toy bricks. They can be assembled to create all kinds of structures, deconstructed and then reconstructed endlessly to make new midnight land mines. The more Lego blocks you have, the more opportunity for creativity you have. With ten blocks, you have a limited set of things you can build. With one hundred, or one thousand blocks, you have nearly unlimited flexibility and creativity.

In the new world of work, where you have to proactively leverage foresight to innovate, building a workforce that looks like Lego blocks—which can be assembled and reconstituted for various business goals and tasks—gives you nimbleness to reinvent your future and withstand the ebbs and flows of a stormy sea.

As with the most complex Lego toy structures that offer instructions on how to assemble the Lego set, you'll need best practices on how to connect the various parts of your workforce to put your foresight to work and innovate through your business model. This chapter is designed to provide you with an outline for building a radically adaptive workforce that is collaborative, inclusive, agile, and resilient. It addresses the three critical questions of what, who, and where, and presents a guide to executing on the plans built from these questions.

To begin, you have to answer three critical questions: First, what work actually needs to be done? Second, how do you decide who does the work? Third, where does it need to get done? At the end of this chapter, we'll explore a fourth corollary question: How do you move your current workforce into this new paradigm?

As we look deeper into each of these questions, we will bring them to life by showing how they apply for different company avatars: for example, a multibillion-dollar multinational company has different needs and will make different decisions than a fast-growing small, twenty-person business would. "Regardless of the size or nature of the business, we find that this playbook is universally applicable to all clients where we have deployed it," said Vijay Murugappan, CEO of First Quadrant Advisory (FQA) and former vice president of strategy at a multibillion-dollar health insurance company.

Our objective in this chapter is twofold: (1) to offer an adaptable framework to organize a work process that could be daunting and (2) to equip you and your team with a common language for continuous transparent dialogue throughout this process.

Before you initiate these steps, however, we recommend a few mission-critical things to set yourself for success. First, don't be afraid to adapt this framework to the reality of your own team and organization. The processes we describe in this chapter are most effective when embedded in your strategic choices, existing workforce, and progress-tracking mechanisms. Second, start with the right team. Cross-functional teams with diverse experiences inside and outside your company are critical. We'll explain later how to build such a cross-functional group. Finally, approach this as an iterative process rather than a one-off large initiative with an expiration date. Let's now dive in systematically to help you design a workforce that will help you, your team, and your organization leap five years forward.

What Work Needs to Be Done?

The late Clay Christensen, a professor at Harvard Business School and best known for his seminal work on disruptive innovation, posited that great companies often fail to innovate because they don't create products or services that fill their customers' real needs, or the "jobs to be done"—which customers hire them to do.[2] As customers, we "hire" (i.e., buy) a product or service to accomplish a certain task for us. If the product or service fails to fill the need, we fire it and hire another. As a leader in your organization, one of your key priorities is to establish what tasks need to be done and who you should hire, literally and figuratively, to get that job done. This first section will describe the process by which you determine what jobs need to be done.

Building the team

Before you even start redesigning your workforce, it's critical to think consciously about who is in the room, and who has a seat at what we like to call the Jedi Task Force. The Lego Group has a long-standing partnership with Lucasfilm, licensing Star Wars characters as Lego building blocks. We found the analogy very fitting, as your workforce transformation team is responsible for assembling the Lego block work "force" of the future.

Work has become increasingly cross-functional. As a result, the knowledge required to understand the dynamics between various tasks is dispersed across various silos within a company. At the same time, the experience required to reimagine new processes is dispersed outside the company and often across industries. For a workforce transformation to be effective, this knowledge asymmetry within transformation teams needs to be addressed.

Mariya Filipova told us that a large part of her ability to deliver quick wins and forward momentum in any meeting is based on who's in the room. "Once I define what we need to get done and the decisions we need to make in the meeting, I spend most of my time thinking about who needs to be in the room to make it happen: the decision-makers and their influencers, the internal experts and the industry outsiders, the vocal enthusiasts and the quiet skeptics. When the balance is just right, there is a certain flow, trust, and momentum in the room—and that's how you know you've got the right people making the right decisions."

Relying solely on your existing team, or internal expertise, has limitations because internal operating teams are often wedded to a certain way of doing things. While your colleagues are deeply experienced in their work, they also have certain unconscious biases about the tasks they complete. Similar to how racehorses have blinders attached to bridles near their eyes—to help them see only what's in front of them and not on anything to their sides or behind them—internal teams are often focused on what's immediately ahead of them and not on orthogonal possibilities. We recommend bringing in fresh eyes to your Jedi Task Force, whether these are external experts you engage as consultants, or internal folks who are not currently tasked on the same project.

At the same time, internal team knowledge plays a critical role in your Jedi Task Force. If your team is solely composed of external experts, they may help you see an exciting future, but they likely lack the institutional awareness to fully comprehend how and why certain things get done. Moreover, external experts lack the internal sponsorship necessary to push through experimentation within the bureaucracy.

So, your optimal Jedi Task Force would be composed of both external experts and internal team members. External experts provide an outsider perspective and can ask the tough questions; internal members generate the institutional knowledge needed to commit to a massive workforce transformation.

Deciding where to focus

Once you have your Jedi Task Force established, it's now time to break down job tasks into their component parts, or microtasks. This step is often the hardest part of the sausage making and can be quite daunting given that any company, whether a small business or a large multinational, has hundreds, if not thousands or even tens of thousands, of processes that make up every workflow. How do you even begin to think about where to start? Which job tasks should be the highest priority for evaluation? We recommend zooming out and looking at the big picture of the company and then applying filters to prioritize where to begin focusing your workforce redesign. Vijay Murugappan suggests applying three filters.

The first filter through which to view this process is a *strategic lens*. Which parts of your business or your team's focus are most aligned to the mission and vision of your organization? The answer will certainly differ for each team and for each company. Ask yourself more specifically these questions: Which parts of your business provide your team with distinct competitive advantage in the marketplace? Which parts of your business differentiate you strategically from your competition? Is it your product? Then start looking at how your product teams operate. Is it your supply chain? Then start looking at how your logistics teams operate. For example, many companies assume that any back-office process such as IT or call center operations should be integrated into a shared services function, if possible. But that shouldn't necessarily be the case; there could be strategic reasons for keeping them distinct and duplicative in function. For instance, a consumer-facing firm that relies on mergers and acquisitions for growth could decide to retain all support functions within its acquired companies rather than consolidating them into a central shared service. This separate-services approach allows the firm to strategically acquire and divest high-performing businesses and maintain maximum flexibility.

The second filter to consider would be a *financial lens*. Which parts of your business or team provide the most revenue or the most profitability to your business? Which parts are the biggest cost centers or cost drivers? Identify two or three financial metrics as variables, and look around your organization to see where it might be more expensive to deliver a particular project than it is to staff that project. Are there redundant or overlapping project teams from different units that focus on the same end goal, but without the strategic reasons Vijay describes above?

A third filter to consider is a *performance lens*, which prioritizes the roles or jobs that provide the highest performance as perceived by the end user, client, or consumer. For example, you might prioritize roles that encourage clients to provide the highest net promoter scores, or marketing roles that build the highest end-consumer loyalty.

The key point here is that the right filters to use will differ for each team, each business, and each industry. Strategy, finance, and performance are merely three lenses to begin narrowing down tens of thousands of job processes and identifying the highest-impact tasks to transform your workforce.

Next, combine the various attributes into a single color-coded heat map, which represents the data graphically. That makes it easy to see at a glance which tasks are in greatest strategic alignment with team goals or which tasks would yield the greatest benefit if they were redesigned. Each heat map is unique to each team and each company and provides an integrated way to help leaders assess priorities, identify gaps between intent, spending, and outcomes, and focus on the highest-impact tasks first. The heat map helps leaders decide which job tasks to prioritize in a first wave of redesign, which tasks to prioritize in a second wave, which to prioritize in a third wave, and so forth, as measured by strategic alignment and the overall benefit of a workforce redesign.

Pixelating and reimagining the job

Once you've identified the top ten, twenty, or fifty job work flows for redesigning through the preceding heat map exercise, it's time to do the nitty-gritty and break down each of the job tasks into their underlying microtasks—a process we call *pixelating* (a reference to photography, where thousands of underlying pixels make up the greater image). You do this by first assembling your Jedi Task Force in one room or virtually online, to systematically discuss each job flow. The goal is to pixelate, or break down, each job workflow into its underlying microtasks and to capture those microtasks on a whiteboard (physical or digital) so everyone can agree on the tasks required for each job to be done.

To pixelate, Vijay suggests answering three questions in a systematic process: What is? What if? What works? We'll describe each of these three questions as a workshop step that needs to be accomplished sequentially.

The time needed to workshop these three steps will depend on your team's resources, size, and bandwidth. For example, a smaller twenty-person company may be able to answer all three questions in a one-day session, whereas a multinational business unit may need several days to workshop the answers to the three questions. The important part is that you approach the process systematically in a three-step process.

Step 1: What is?

What is the current state of your team or company's work processes? Start by convening your Jedi Task Force and documenting each of the tasks in your workflow step-by-step. Vinay Nadig, who leads First Quadrant Advisory's Transformation practice, explained how a multibillion-dollar health-care insurer followed this three-step process to reduce medical claim processing time in a specific business unit. The company first convened a Jedi Task Force of forty employees to document all the various existing steps in this process. This cross-functional group of executives, operations staff, and subject matter experts used their varied experiences and perspectives to reveal how claim processing was actually done—not how it was supposed to be done. To their surprise, they identified 132 steps to process and reimburse a claim—some of which were 100 percent manual and not documented in any standard operating procedure. They captured these steps visually on a virtual whiteboard.

They then asked, "Why is this being done?" The goal was to identify the constraints or requirements that have shaped the current workflow and to eliminate the barriers deemed duplicative, non-value-adding,
or otherwise wasteful. In some instances, the answer was because a technology gap existed or a system limitation caused the process to be done
manually. In other instances, a gap in personnel training or knowledge
necessitated the action. By the end of this step, the Jedi Task Force identified forty-two barriers in the existing workflow and categorized
them as people, process, and technology constraints (although you
should not limit yourself to these three categories if other categories
are relevant for your team and organization). In the next steps, the team
would test possible solutions for these barriers.

Step 2: What if?

In this step, your Jedi Task Force should focus on this question: how do
we ideally want it to be done? The goal is to first design the end state
of your workflow, without any constraints on technology, time, or
resources. And then map this end-state vision against the requirements
and constraints identified in the first workshop step. This matching of
a future vision with real constraints provides an optimal solution set. In
the preceding health-care insurer example, executives found this step
challenging. Many years of execution and focus on quarterly results ran
counter to unconstrained thinking. This is where having external
experts on your Jedi Task Force will be helpful. External advisers with
cross-industry exposure to what has worked successfully for other companies, what has failed, and the circumstances driving success or failure
can help your internal executive team think more imaginatively about
how to build a workflow without constraints.

Step 3: What works?

In this final step, your Jedi Task Force needs to answer this question:
How do we make the change last? How do we develop solutions that

can be adopted at scale within three months, six months, or a year? Your task force begins by discussing barriers to change, generating ideas, and assessing the feasibility of each proposed resolution. In the health-care insurance example, the resolutions were grouped into four mutually exclusive areas: resolve now, "phone a friend," commit to resolve, and defer.

Some barriers could be resolved immediately by asking the people in the room to make decisions and commit to them right then and there. For example, two department heads decided to eliminate an interde-partmental approval process and cut two weeks out of what had been an eight-week work process. In another example, a different set of lead-ers committed on the spot to jointly invest $50,000 from their collec-tive budgets to make a systemic change. For some barriers, they had to "phone a friend," as the people who needed to make a decision weren't in the room, and the task force was able to resolve the problem imme-diately on the phone with the decision-making party.

In some cases, the resolution could not be done on the spot, so the team agreed that these barriers must be resolved and committed to a timeline for resolution. And finally, the team deferred on some barriers that either were not worth resolving (e.g., the solutions were too expen-sive to implement and created insufficient value) or could not be resolved (e.g., the solutions needed legal or regulatory fixes).

Coming out of these three pixelating steps, the health-care insur-ance team eliminated thirty-two process steps immediately and identi-fied an additional eighteen steps for elimination in the subsequent two weeks. Three months later, the time needed to process medical claims from start to finish was reduced from eight weeks to nineteen days—a 66 percent reduction in time and steps needed to accomplish the task!

Reengineering behavior

Once you've gone through the pixelation exercise just described, you may decide that your existing workforce can do some of these tasks but that the team needs to change its current behaviors to accomplish those tasks. You have to go through a similar pixelation exercise to answer the following questions: What are the old behaviors? What are the new necessary behaviors to succeed in these jobs? And how do we train our team to develop and adopt these highest-return behaviors?

One way to pixelate behaviors is to start by defining a clear goal. First, assemble your team and ask what behaviors need to be demonstrated by the team, collectively and individually, for the team to accomplish that goal. You may not be aware of what your current behaviors are, so it may be helpful to bring in a coach to help observe behaviors. Identify the behaviors clearly: the old behavior was X, the new behavior is Y. Second, be very specific and ask who needs to change their actions for the team to succeed. How will the team members drive each other to keep each other accountable for new behaviors? How can they give each other feedback? Finally, make sure *you* are the first domino to change. Volunteer to be the first person to describe what *your* old behaviors and new behaviors are, so that your team can model the exercise correctly.

This pixelation process can feel tedious, but it's a necessary first step in redesigning your workforce. If you follow the three-step "What is?" "What if?" and "What works?" workshop methodology just described, you'll be able to understand what each job flow requires. And you'll be able to decide how to reassemble the tasks, figure which highest-value behaviors need to be developed, and then staff those job tasks appropriately with the right Lego block. Deciding on the appropriate workforce is where we turn our attention to next.

What Workforce Will We Engage?

Once you've pixelated the various priority jobs to be done within your team and your organization and pixelated them into their constituent microtasks, you now have to decide who will do the work. How do you decide if you should build, buy, or borrow that talent? By this ques-

FIGURE 7-1

Workforce decision dials

DIAL 1: AUGMENTATION

Human   Algorithmic

DIAL 2: EMPLOYMENT

Traditional   Gig

DIAL 3: ECOSYSTEM

Internal   External

tion, we mean, should you expend the effort to develop the workforce internally, buy the talent externally through vendor partnerships, or borrow the talent through third-party labor platforms?

To decide which Lego blocks to assemble for your workforce, consider this visual of two knobs, or dials, on a car radio (a predigital car radio!). We call them *decision dials*. One dial on the right side of the radio tunes the frequency, and the other knob on the left changes the volume. Depending on how you move these dials, you can change the musical experience in your car: what you hear and how loudly you hear it.

We believe each company will need to make six decisions along the two main dimensions of workforce and workplace. The first three decisions focus on *who* does the work, which we'll explore in this section (figure 7-1). The second three focus on *where* the work is done, which we'll explore in the following section. How you dial each set of knobs will dictate the workforce you design and the Lego blocks you assemble. Each ending solution is unique to each company. There is no categorical right or wrong answer, but there is a solution unique to each set of strategic priorities and cultural value sets.

Let's consider how Paul Hlivko approached this first dimension of workforce design. Paul is the chief technology and experience officer of Wellmark Blue Cross Blue Shield, a health-care insurer based in Iowa. Wellmark faced a triple whammy in 2020: a global pandemic, a key partner's computer system was knocked offline for weeks, and a massive multistate windstorm called a derecho struck one of its primary markets. So it's natural to assume that Wellmark's workforce was impacted in 2020. It *was* affected, but not to the extent that other organizations were, because Paul's team had relied on a blended workforce model, where many of the contributors on his team are nontraditional and work across the globe via crowdsourcing.

In 2020, Paul's team engaged more than 150 crowd workers, located in fifty countries, through the company's crowdsourcing platform partner TopCoder. These on-demand workers helped in a variety of traditional software tasks like user experience design, engineering, and development. But Paul's team also used the platform to identify hard-to-source talent like data science skills, which are in top demand, regardless of where they live. This crowd labor platform not only gave Wellmark the added benefit of a twenty-four-hour globally distributed workforce but also added a layer of agility to help Paul balance the workforce demands when his on-site teams were hindered by local events.

"Of all the talent challenges Wellmark faced in 2020, the crowd was the only workforce model that did not have some amount of downtime," said Paul. Crowd labor reinforced the company's resilience, as the diversity of locations, skill sets, and talent on their crowdsourcing platform lowered the likelihood of workforce disruption. Similar to how cloud infrastructure providers—like Amazon Web Services—lower the potential for technology failure through their sheer density and number of data centers, crowd labor platforms can lower labor disruption risks, especially when they are leveraged at scale.

Crowd talent is a great way to empower one person internally and help them scale their work. But it wasn't a staff replacement strategy for Wellmark. "This isn't about labor cost leverage. It's about getting the best minds in our company and the world to help us drive the best outcomes for our clients and members," Paul said. He prioritized keeping key differentiating skills, like customer experience, digital, engineering, and cloud infrastructure, inside the firm. But he also believed there was plenty of opportunity to plug in crowds to his existing teams and add diversity of ideas and experiences to those internal teams so they could develop the best and most creative solutions possible. "From the beginning," he said, "we treated the crowd as a shared service team that anyone could access. They operated like any other team in our shared services portfolio. We even gave the crowd a scrum name, to reinforce that ordinariness and inclusivity, so that everyone knew the crowd team was just like another internal team."

Fast-forward five years, and Paul expects to expand Wellmark's usage of crowdsourcing platforms to provide talent in additional verticals besides software development. "To succeed in our workforce strategy," Paul said, "we need to continue supporting a culture that focuses on ideas and outcomes over how people choose to be employed, while investing in our internal teams to keep learning new skills, like how to partner with distributed talent. It's good for our team members' personal development and careers, and it's good for the company's agility and resilience."

Speaking of five years forward, what time frame are you envisioning for your future preferred workforce state? Earlier in this book, we outlined a five-year-forward preferred future state for your business. So for the sake of consistency, your workforce dials should reflect this five-year-forward ending state. For now, don't preoccupy yourself with how you get your team or organization's workforce to this future state. Focus on establishing what the ideal workforce would look like when you achieve your preferred future state in five years, and that will serve as a goal for developing a road map for the actual workforce transformation, which we'll cover later in this chapter.

As the future of work drives toward a segmentation of tasks, we'll see more diversity in where work is done and who does that work, as we saw in Paul's case. To succeed in building their Lego blocks, team leaders will need to make three critical workforce decisions. Remember, there is no universal one right answer, but it is important to consider these questions conscientiously: How do we augment our employees with technology? How do we make the most of the people who do not work in our team, department, company or industry? How do we optimize my relationships with partners and collaborators?

Dial 1. Augmentation: Human or algorithmic?

For the better part of the last decade, Hollywood, and Silicon Valley have hyped fears about how robots and algorithms will make human jobs obsolete once the singularity arrives. Of course, we know this not to be true—at least not yet!—but there are glimmers of truth to that science fiction future that we should explore.

The truth is, work in the future will be a balance between human intervention and automated technologies. The future of human work will rely on creativity, not productivity. Work that is repetitive, dirty, and dangerous will more than likely become automated through robotics and algorithms. Work that requires higher-order creativity, complex problem-solving, collaboration, communication, and emotional intelligence will be the domain of humans.

AI algorithms have developed swiftly over the last few years, and many repetitive and basic tasks can now be digitized and performed by natural-language processing, machine learning, and other AI technologies. Inviting an expert in these technologies to join your Jedi Task Force can help you decide what algorithmic technologies exist now, and how they can realistically help you augment your workflow over the next five years, when you achieve your preferred future state. Instead of doing work the same way you have always been doing through repetitive data entry and data manipulation, let AI technologies augment your human endeavors.

Vinay Nadig illustrates how the human and machine model works in practice. Onboarding large corporate customers is a constant challenge for health insurers. The combination of legacy systems, manual activities, and heavily customized product offerings poses significant challenges. This frequently results in elongated onboarding cycle times, inconsistent data quality, and, ultimately, delayed service for the patient as the end user. Patients often experience delays in getting prescriptions filled, in scheduling procedures, and in getting approval for surgeries.

In this situation, recruiting automation technology like AI and software algorithms to simplify the onboarding process was a no-brainer for the health insurer in Vinay's example. But servicing strategic accounts in the highly complex world of health insurance benefits is still a high-touch business. It requires years of relationship experience and a deep and nuanced understanding of customer needs and internal capabilities. Vinay led an initiative to develop what his team called *cobots*—a software robot that would collaborate with a human worker to accomplish a task. To prepare customer orders for the insurer's core systems, an unattended software robot was able to use algorithms to automate much of the front-end order entry process. But instead of finalizing orders automatically, the robot nudges an experienced human worker to check the order for nuances, complexities, and other "gotchas" that the robot's algorithms might miss. The robot reduced repetitive tasks and rote work, resulting in significant savings in time and labor. It also freed up human employees to engage in more critical, knowledge-based roles, and higher-touch tasks of servicing customers and creating customer delight.

This level of augmentation will depend on the specifics of your company and industry. The various AI technologies available now are not designed to replace your workforce. But rather, AI as a Lego block of your workforce can accelerate value creation for your company while freeing up your staff to focus on higher-order, higher-value knowledge work.

Finally, as you evaluate the various work streams and jobs that need to be done, and as you ask yourself if this work should be done by a human or an algorithm, ask yourself, does it even *need* to be done? Part of this pixelation and workforce redesign process involves making sure you don't hire the right person to do the wrong job. Step back and ask, "Does this task or unit of activity even need to exist?" If it doesn't, eliminate the task and move on.

Dial 2. Employment: Traditional or gig?

For almost one hundred years since the Great Depression of the 1930s, governments and labor movements worldwide have pushed for the safeguarding of full-time employment as a means to create more equitable and stable societies. This social contract remained stable until the Great Recession of 2008, when the coincidental convergence of mobile phone technologies, mass connectivity, and widespread unemployment led citizens to take up any gig project to earn money through small tasks. This new gig economy—also known as the sharing economy—tapped into a deep well of underutilized assets, from unused private bedrooms for short-term rental on platforms like Airbnb, to private cars for shared taxi service on transportation networks like Uber and Lyft. These gig workers occupy a new job category that many companies have come to rely on as a supplemental labor force. The workers are not full-time employees, and they are not traditional freelance contracted consultants. Rather, these individuals work on short-term projects, depending on the level of complexity of the task at hand. Paul Hlivko's crowd labor model at Wellmark is a good example of this contingent gig economy.

We anticipate the technological trends that sparked the sharing economy over the last decade to continue growing exponentially over the coming years. Through the efforts of companies like SpaceX and Virgin Orbit, most of America will be connected online through microsatellites by 2025, providing low-bandwidth internet connectivity for all Americans, rural and urban. This connectivity will increase access to digital services for underserved populations and will reinforce the development of a fully digital labor market where anyone can work anywhere, on any type of remote work, on any task. Other companies are working on similar low-bandwidth satellite connectivity for the rest of the world. As a result, we should expect to see another three billion individuals newly connected online by the end of the 2020s. Now imagine tapping into the cognitive genius of anyone on the planet to get any gig project done. That's an extraordinary resource!

Indeed, brilliant people are everywhere, and not just located near your corporate headquarters. Bill Joy, the cofounder of Sun Microsystems, once said, "The smartest people always work for someone else."[3] It's true. The smartest people don't *all* work at Amazon. Or Apple. Or Google. Or General Motors. Or Walmart. Or any other company. They work for all kinds of organizations all over the world. The most successful leaders must figure out how to tap into the cognitive intelligence of this distributed workforce and bring that intelligence into their businesses. And crowd-driven gig platforms can help build this radical adaptability for a new world of work.

These platforms have popped up in many disciplines to connect a distributed labor pool with this global demand for talent. They have become trusted platforms for many companies and verticals that are seeking workers for a variety of services, from the more mundane, simple tasks like data entry to more complex white-collar expert services like accounting and law and even higher-order creative disciplines like ideation and design. Among these platforms are Tongal for creative advertising, TopCoder for software development, Workrise for skilled trades and energy fieldwork, and Upwork for general freelance work.

American government policy is starting to support this gig ecosystem and solidify gig work in the new economy. In 2020, a majority of the citizens of California voted to create a new labor category for gig workers, distinct from full-time employment and independent freelance work. This new labor policy provides specific gig workers with a hybrid arrangement of job benefits, lying somewhere between full-time employment and freelance status. As we've found with many innovations coming out of California, we'll probably see this labor policy trend continue across the country.

So how do you decide if your workforce should be based on a traditional full-time employee model, a gig-economy model, or a hybrid somewhere in between the two? How do you tune the decision dials? The answer will depend on your team, your business, your industry, and your preferred future state. There is no one right answer but only an answer that is right for you.

But we do know that there are some *wrong* answers to avoid. Certainly, anyone who is a critical part of your business's competitive advantage (whether that's products, supply chain, marketing, etc.) should be a full-time employee so you have direction over their workflow. For example, specialists who are critical to your business should be internal hires. They help differentiate your business from the competition. As another example, tiger teams, which are tasked with finding new pathways of innovation for your organization, should be fully internal employees, as you'll want to harness all their innovation energies and not let your competitors get similar benefits from them.

Which roles should be performed by gig workers? We argue that any task can be dialed up on the gig knob if it is repetitive, not core to your business, does not need consistent direction over how the work is done, and can be done by workers who don't require internal firm knowledge.

Dial 3. Ecosystem: Internal or external?

The natural inclination for many organizations has historically been to hire an individual, whether full time or part time, to accomplish a particular task. This practice continues to be a predominant workforce model for many organizations. But it's not the only one. In addition to gig work performed by freelance individuals, companies can also partner with third-party organizations to accomplish a variety of tasks. These organizations can be fully outsourced staffing firms, supply-chain vendors, or even other partners in the corporate ecosystem.

Consider this example of a manufacturing company that has tremendous variability in seasonal demand and explores how to work with its ecosystem partners to create a more sustainable workforce. Mike Clementi, executive vice president of HR at Unilever, is experimenting with a shared-talent platform between the company's ecosystem partners. Because of the seasonality of its manufacturing, Unilever faces volume spikes that it needs to staff up and then staff down for, seasonally. But if it could partner with other companies that also have seasonality in their workforces—albeit at different times of the year—Unilever could create stable year-round jobs for employees, who would cycle through different companies based on need and be reskilled for each task. This approach reframes the narrative from cost-cutting and outsourcing seasonal employment to a more sustainable shared workforce that extends impact throughout society. "Think of it as an API [application programming interface] for talent," Mike said. "You can plug into the API for when you need its resources."

How do you decide whether certain tasks should be executed internally or externally? The level of control needed to deliver a particular customer result should guide this decision. If the task is dependent on other variables that are internally managed, then that task will likely not be accomplished externally as efficiently. However, if the task can be done with minimal to no direction from management and is independent of internal controls, then it would suggest a good example for external work staffing.

As we've said before, and it bears repeating, there is no *one* right answer to this decision dial. The right configuration will depend on your particular organization. For example, a small manufacturing company with $20 million in revenue would likely make different decisions than a $5 billion multinational corporation would on how to turn the workforce decision dials. Both decisions are valid, for their enterprises. The right tuning will depend on where you are now and where you want to be in your preferred future state in five years.

Where Will the Workforce Work?

The next three decision dials focus on your workplace and will help you determine where your workforce should be located, and the optimal setting where processes and work tasks should be accomplished: in the office, remotely, in-country, offshore, in open environments, or in closed environments (figure 7-2).

Consider the case of Igor Institute, a twenty-five-person engineering consultancy based in Seattle and founded in 2013. Igor Institute designs and engineers hardware for consumer electronics and medical device companies, focusing on product leadership, mechanical, electrical, and firmware engineering. Hardware designers tend to be an extroverted group, constantly tinkering with toys, and Igor's office is a fun

FIGURE 7-2

Workplace decision dials

DIAL 4: PRESENCE

In-person	Remote

DIAL 5: LOCATION

Onshore	Offshore

DIAL 6: ENVIRONMENT

Open	Closed

place to be, with pianos, drums, and guitars strewn around the office, reflecting the founders' personality.

When the pandemic arrived in mid-March 2020, Aren Kaser, Igor's CEO and cofounder, sent his team home to shelter in place and work remotely. For the next four months, the team worked from home via a variety of online collaboration tools, and things seemed to be working relatively well. But by midsummer, Aren called a team meeting. He felt that something was off and that project deadlines were getting unusually hectic.

Because the pandemic had made in-person collaboration impossible, virtual brainstorming and problem-solving took longer. These activities took more steps and more time, and were asynchronous rather than synchronous. Something that would ordinarily be an easy thing to do in the office—like ask a colleague for input, as in, "Hey, how would you handle this project?" Or "Have you experienced this situation before?"—became much harder to discuss via text, messenger, or email when a person was working remotely. In such an environment, the barrier to communication was higher—surprising, given all the various communication tools available—because it felt more vulnerable to type out "I need help" and have that thread live online forever than it felt to say casually to a colleague in the office at the water cooler, "I have no idea how to do that; what do you think?" Saying it orally required less commitment.

When the team was working collaboratively in person, its goal was clearly focused on product and client success. But when people were working at home, the goal shifted a little and became about the ability to solve the problem on your own, without asking for help. The business effect was that team projects were getting delayed by slowed communication. Even a few days' worth of delays would pile up and push the team to the edge of immovable client deadlines. This rarely happened when the staff was working in person at the office before the pandemic.

So at a virtual staff meeting midsummer, Aren mandated that team members should feel comfortable to call each other daily, interrupt their colleagues' workday, and force engagement, since it's easy to ignore text messages, emails, or other internal communication tools. A two-minute conversation could save an entire day of individual research. "We need to be OK with disrupting people at times, while working virtually," he said. By the end of 2020, this small shift in team communication helped Igor power to a 32 percent increase in revenue year on year, far outpacing its peer group in an otherwise very difficult year.

Going into 2021, Aren anticipated that the post-Covid environment meant a hybrid work policy. But rather than an arbitrary days-per-week policy in the office, the company needed to figure out a policy for when to work in the office during particularly collaboration-intense phases of a project—like phase 1 architecting or phase 2 prototyping—while other, later phases of project execution could be done virtually and with less intense collaboration. During the early phases of a project, it was exponentially more powerful to have senior engineers from multiple disciplines in one room, since that's what the company is in the business of doing: making things that have never been made before and overcoming new engineering challenges daily.

The lesson to take away from Igor Institute is the need to consciously choose your work environment, depending on the type of project that is being staffed. If your team needs to tinker, collaborate, and communicate, the ideal environment is an open space, in the office, or at a geographically convenient pop-up work outpost. If your team needs to focus independently, a closed office environment would be preferable, possibly at home or remote elsewhere.

The key questions to consider include these: Should our employees be working onsite, or remotely? And if they work remotely, how can we ensure they are engaged virtually? If our employees work off-site, how can we take advantage of opportunities presented by different time zones, different geographic locations, and the lower cost of labor off-shore? Finally, what is the optimal environment to encourage productivity and well-being? Is it in an open environment like the open-plan offices of the pre-pandemic age or a closed environment that encourages deep focus?

Dial 4. Presence: In-person or remote?

The professional story of 2020 surely was the mandated push to *work from home* (WFH), as the coronavirus pandemic shut down in-person businesses all over the world and forced companies to adopt remote work practices. Whether the WFH movement is a momentary blip in work history remains to be seen, but organizations' previous rationale for having to be physically colocated has definitely shifted. Prior to the pandemic, only a small percentage of full-time corporate employees worked from home or remotely, and they did so because they had specific personal or family reasons to do so. But the pandemic forced a decentralization of all knowledge jobs that were previously resistant to remote work, whether for cultural, technical, or organizational reasons. And it showed that teams could be even *more* innovative, collaborative, and productive while remote, *if* they instituted some of the high-return leadership practices we described in the first half of this book.

In the new world of work post-pandemic, it's clear that many jobs can indeed be done remotely and that there are few tasks that absolutely need to be done in the office. A recent research study by freelance gig platform Upwork suggests that more than 36 million Americans will permanently work remotely by 2025, representing almost 25 percent of the entire US workforce. How you tune the decision dials for in-person versus remote work will depend largely on your organizational circumstances, values, and preferences. But the decision dial is not an either-or decision. It can be a hybrid of both.

In addition to your existing in-person team, having a partly hybrid team or a fully remote one can open your organization to tapping into the cognitive intelligence of the world, regardless of where people are located. You can expand your flexibility in hiring, and find the best person for the task, whether they are local, in Memphis or Mumbai. Location doesn't matter, as long as they have an internet connection and can use online collaboration tools to interact effectively with their remote and in-person colleagues.

Tomes will be written on best practices for remote and hybrid work. Some companies may designate some weeks or days as in-person time, encouraging in-person collaboration and culture building, as described with the Igor Institute example. Others will choose different policies and priorities. Our goal here isn't to be absolutely proscriptive, as different companies will have different needs. But before deciding where to tune the decision dial, we recommend identifying *why* you need to have your team work in person, and then balance that against the benefits of operating remotely. Is it necessary for team building? Is it necessary for serendipitous hallway interactions? Or is it because that's just how you always operated pre-pandemic? We believe you can engineer for any of these results by conscientiously and purposefully designing the *right* hybrid work structure for your organization. For example, you can default to virtual meetings to maximize collaboration and inclusion and have hundreds of employees involved in innovation, rather than let the size of a physical room or the cost of a large gathering dictate how many people can participate in innovation or an important conversation. And on the flip side, you can design in-person events at the office to achieve specific team goals, like fostering one-on-one personal connections, or schedule casual group hangouts. If you're purposeful about designing your hybrid work structure, you can maximize radical adaptability at the organizational level through a hybrid model. The key here is to be *purposeful*.

The benefits of hybrid and remote work are real: it can help you reimagine your real estate footprint, reduce your overall administrative costs, and simultaneously increase employee wellness as they balance personal and family responsibilities. It can also help you win the war for talent in a hypercompetitive labor pool. The ongoing length of the pandemic gave many employees a taste and an appreciation of flexible work, and many are unwilling to give it up and go back to the way things were pre-pandemic. If employees are consumers of jobs—which they are in a growing economy—there's a real argument to be made that hybrid work structures can be used as a tool to attract and retain talent. Indeed, a hybrid workplace structure will be a source of tremendous competitive advantage in this new world of work.

Finally, as we look to the future, we can see that new technologies—such as previously discussed avatar systems, virtual and augmented reality, and spatial web—will continue to evolve and make physical location even less important. We'll soon be able to leverage these new technologies to make hybrid collaboration and communication even more effective and effortless. Employees will demand it. Technology will allow it. And the labor market will respond. So *now* is the time to consider how you optimize for this hybrid future, because it's inevitable.

Dial 5. Location: Onshore or offshore?

You might decide that labor cost savings are a critical part of your strategic advantage and that the best way to do that would be to move certain tasks offshore, to jurisdictions with lower labor costs. Or you might consider that having staff overseas in different time zones would give you a longer workday and a leg up on your competition, since your offshore workers can work while you sleep, and vice versa. Offshoring has been a major trend in big business for the last three decades, as globalization lowered barriers to trade and as internet technologies allowed for seamless global communication between corporate headquarters and offshore labor markets. It's certainly a model that will stay around. To what extent offshoring works for you depends on your needs and goals.

On the other hand, you might decide that your supply chain is a critical part of your competitive advantage and that an unexpected disruption to that supply chain—as was evident in the coronavirus pandemic, when national borders were closed to trade—would be devastating to your business. Labor may be less expensive offshore, but the risk, and potential cost, to your business if that supply chain were disrupted would offset lower labor costs offshore. So you may want to instead prioritize bringing your key supply-chain partners back onshore, or near your home-market shore, to minimize disruption risks.

As with the previous decision dials, the choice between onshore and offshore talent will depend on your organizational values, circumstances, and preferences. At Ferrazzi Greenlight, we experimented in 2020 with offshoring part of our administrative work, which everyone on staff hated doing. We weren't sure if the experiment would work out and if lag times between full-time staff in the United States and freelance staff offshore would complicate our workflow. But the results pleasantly surprised us. We are a small company, with a dozen full-time employees. Three of these employees are associates making about $85,000 per year. They are very talented in their work and client delivery, but they uniformly fell flat on accomplishing the necessary administrative tasks, like data entry and data tagging—possibly because there just weren't enough hours in the day. Or the task was tedious, and they wanted to prioritize higher-value work. We decided to hire offshore virtual assistants based in Guatemala for each of these employees to reduce the administrative burden for them and free up their time to focus on higher-value client work. By year's end, the three associates had become more productive than ever before, and we had created sustainable work for three virtual assistants abroad. A win-win for all.

Dial 6. Environment: Open or closed?

The final consideration for where your work stream can be accomplished is whether the work can be best done in an open, collaborative environment or in a closed, focused environment. If your work needs to be done synchronously—one task after the other—or needs a careful orchestration of multiple inputs, then an open, collaborative environment might be the best choice. Conversely, if your work can be done independently of other tasks, without input from other dependencies, or in a nonlinear fashion and at any time, then this particular task may be best suited to a more focused, closed environment. It's not a strictly binary decision. While some knowledge jobs can be done independently and remotely, they may need to tap into short-term in-person team collaboration. This collaboration doesn't necessarily mean meeting at corporate HQ but could occur at a local co-working facility or a pop-up office outpost geographically convenient to team members.

Execute the Transition

Earlier in this chapter, we suggested you should not preoccupy yourself with *how* to change your workforce composition until you have clarity on the six decision dials establishing what the work is, who does it, and where it's done. Now it's time to cross that bridge to the promised land. How do you move toward that preferred Lego block workforce? And what should you consider in deciding how to manage and train your various teams and workforces?

Once you have determined the optimal positioning of the decision dials for your organization, we recommend running a small test, what Mariya Filipova calls a scalable win (SWIN) to validate the choices in the reality of day-to-day operations. Similar to how startups build MVPs to quickly determine if their product or offering has legs in the marketplace, a SWIN takes the preferred future state for your workforce and runs small, targeted *tests* or milestones to determine if this new workflow can indeed be done remotely, asynchronously, or offshore. Each SWIN is designed to validate an assumption or meet a requirement for adoption at scale. A successful SWIN would reveal barriers to deployment early, or turn into a bigger SWIN and ultimately a phased rollout. Its success is measured by a subgrouping of your Jedi Task Force to evaluate that specific workflow. A SWIN can be as small as getting a buy-in from a key decision-maker on a call, or as large as launching a new algorithm to automate a critical process. The important thing is that SWINs build on each other to get you closer to the desired outcome.

"We needed a way to avoid the 'death by pilots' reality that many new ideas fall into," Mariya said, recalling the effort it took to go from a choice on the decision dial to putting that decision into practice. "Some SWINs cascaded into enterprise-wide initiatives and prepared us for successful deployment at scale. Others didn't take off and allowed us to learn quickly. We considered both types successful."

During her time as vice president of innovation, Mariya launched a number of SWINs to move closer to the end state on the aforementioned decision dials. One of the SWINs resulted in scaling algorithms in call centers that predicted who was likely to call and instead proactively reached out to the customer and offered potential solutions. This augmented call center model increased caller satisfaction and freed up capacity for humans to take on questions that required more complex connections, deeper empathy, and creative solutions.

Once you have tuned the decision dials to your optimal workforce, you now have to start moving in that direction. But strategy does not live in a vacuum. As Peter Drucker once said, "Culture eats strategy for breakfast." What he meant is that no matter how great your strategy, unless you have a cultural transformation process that takes into account the human factors within your company, your strategy will fail. You have to corral culture, learning and development, and incentive structures to move your organization's workforce to your desired vision.

So, what cultural and human capital considerations should you take into account as you build your Lego block workforce? While the specifics of each company will differ according to size, history, industry, and resources, we want to offer you some critical questions to ask and help guide your team to the future. This by no means is meant to be exhaustive, as books will be written on each of the following workforce considerations, but these questions are thought starters for further investigation.

How to train the Lego blocks of the workforce

Most complex Lego toy sets have a base plate where you can plug and play the various Lego blocks. This base plate—namely, the learning and development (L&D) organization—is how the various Lego blocks of your workforce plug into a shared firmwide knowledge base. As the pandemic forced everyone online, it also forced a true democratization of corporate learning: anyone can access any learning through the cloud. Jeff Miller, principal at leadership development firm SSCA told us, "Learning and development is morphing into a true collaboration space. The L&D of the future doesn't create content as much as it used to but rather serves as a platform to facilitate learning through collaboration, conversation, and co-creation." The key is to transform your L&D organization into this base plate that different parts of your Lego blocks can tap into for the information and connection they need to complete a task.

And as the speed of change accelerates, L&D has to help you get to this future, faster, through AI-driven learning algorithms. "We have to go from providing just-in-time skill learning to right-ahead-of-time skill learning," said Miller. As you take more skill development courses online, the most effective learning management systems will make recommendations on what you should learn next, similar to how Netflix or YouTube make video recommendations. But since no one learns exactly the same way, task-based learning will need to be personalized to accommodate different personality types.

Beyond specific skill training, organizations also need to expand the cross-functional nature of skill development to facilitate collaboration and communication between the various Lego blocks. Gone are the days when engineers needed to stick solely to an engineering curriculum. Today, we see engineers collaborating with creatives and functional experts to redefine products and end-user experiences, just as different-colored Lego blocks come together to build new structures. As work becomes more fluid between Lego blocks, L&D leaders will need to make sure their approach to learning is cross-platform so that the various layers can communicate and collaborate with each other effectively.

This continuous-learning model will be a feature of all the most successful organizations. But since we often learn the most through mentorship and informal learning with our colleagues rather than formal classroom training, and since it's more difficult to gather around a virtual water cooler than one in the office, you must also consciously design opportunities for informal learning and mentorship. In this way, the various parts of your Lego block workforce can tap into the aggregate knowledge base.

How to assess the performance of the Lego blocks

For the better part of the last century, organizations have measured employee performance at regular intervals, often annually or semiannually, to determine promotion and pay. Performance reviews are hated by both managers and employees. In the last decade, it became more fashionable in management science to hold informal, frequent, and just-in-time feedback. For example, in 2012, the software company Adobe stopped annual performance reviews altogether, noting that annual assessments were irrelevant in an agile work environment that required continuous improvement.

Given how hard it is to assess performance in a traditional work environment, how do you design a performance and assessment system in a

Lego block workforce where people work in different conditions, environments, and incentive structures? And where physical presence cannot equate to productivity? In the pandemic, the playing field wasn't level when it came to WFH. Some had kids to teach at home, some had to be caregivers at home, while some were alone without distractions. Performance assessment couldn't be measured the same as when everyone showed up every day to an office, where work was "visible." And when face time no longer became necessary for productivity, what mattered was results and meeting business and team objectives.

The specifics of performance assessment will differ for different parts of the Lego block workforce and lie beyond the scope of this book, but overall, performance assessment needs to fundamentally shift from measuring accountability for past actions to a future that measures how quickly your team learns new skills to accomplish a new task. Your role as a leader designing a Lego block workforce is to make sure your team has the necessary resources—from individualized learning and mentorship to clear communication channels—so that they can meet your organizational objectives, regardless of where people are physically located.

How to reskill your existing Lego blocks

You already have a skilled workforce that most likely works for you full time and, up until the pandemic, probably mostly on the premises. Without radical disruption, it's impossible to suddenly move the dial from one extreme to another, as we saw in the early days of the pandemic. So you have to consider how to move your existing workforce to where you ultimately want it to be. As part of that process, you will definitely have employees whom you want to retain but whom you need to reskill for new roles and jobs that fit in your new strategy. By pixelating existing roles into tasks, as described earlier in this chapter, you can identify the skills needed for each job and then help your existing team upskill and make the transition into these new roles. Not everyone will want to retrain for new roles or skills; some people will choose to find new opportunities elsewhere. That's a natural part of every transformation, but you have to be prepared to use your existing workforce to the extent possible.

Consider this example of what we mean. When the pandemic arrived, all retail stores were suddenly closed in the initial nationwide lockdown. The closures impacted both large companies and small companies alike. At outdoor clothing retailer Patagonia, the leadership had to make a quick decision on what to do with its existing retail workforce, which could no longer operate in-store because of mandated closures. At the same time, the company started experiencing a huge increase in e-commerce and online customer service requests, so the leadership team made a critical decision to reskill their in-store sales staff to provide online customer service work, remotely at home. By doing so, Patagonia could retain its existing in-store workforce and reskill them for tasks that were more urgently needed.

Dean Carter, head of global HR for Patagonia, told us, "We've learned a lot during this new way of working. We found that with training, many workers could upskill. We also learned that not all customer service representatives liked face-to-face interactions with customers, and many retail associates preferred helping customers in person." As a result, Patagonia now has a field of flexible employees ready for both in-person retail and online customer service roles. "As our business is seasonal," Dean said, "this gives us a level of flexibility and agility that wouldn't have been possible before. We were able to save jobs and at the same time give our colleagues the opportunity of having two different career paths, in retail and customer service."

Reskilling is especially important in certain industries and geographic locations where there aren't enough new people to hire, so it may be critical to reskill those you already have in-house. Studies show, however, that most employees are dissatisfied with reskilling if it doesn't expand their opportunities for advancement or better pay. One global survey conducted by Massachusetts Institute of Technology showed that 74 percent of respondents believe developing new skills is "strategically important in their organization," but less than a third said they were rewarded for developing new skills. The gap between the two numbers is expressed in worker disengagement. In the survey, 45 percent of employees would be glad to receive a buyout from their employer and take their skills elsewhere.

Underlying Patagonia's ability to reskill its workforce is the company's exceptional reputation as a great place to work. Beyond all the expected perks, pay, and other benefits that distinguish a good employer, Patagonia's explicit purpose statement, "to save our home planet," gives employees a unique sense of belonging and esprit de corps, a feeling that their employer is dedicated to something larger than maximizing profit. Chapter 8 will show how this kind of organizational purpose, when felt and owned by all the company's employees and stakeholders, enhances your organization's competitive advantage to succeed in the new world of work.

GUIDING QUESTIONS
How to Compete in the New World of Work

What combination of a Lego block workforce will give us lasting competitive advantage?

The first step in a workforce redesign is to pixelate existing jobs into tasks to be done and to determine which work streams deserve attention and prioritization from a strategic, financial, and client impact. A three-step workshop methodology of asking "What is?" "What if?" and "What works?" can help leaders reevaluate workforce assumptions to compete in a new world of work.

How do we decide who does the work and how, where, and when it should be done in the future?

Radically adaptable companies leverage six decision dials to systematically assess how work is done, who does the work, and where it's done. New technologies, combined with the experience of remote work in the pandemic, offer new pathways for building a hyperflexible workforce of the future. The most successful organizations will purposefully design and institute hybrid teams to take advantage of the benefits of both remote and in-person work.

Supercharge Your Purpose

W hen our friend Simon Mulcahy, executive vice president and chief innovation officer at Salesforce, was told that the final chapter of this book would be about organizational purpose, he joked that he might not want to participate in the project. "Purpose isn't some afterthought to end a book on an emotional note," he said. "At Salesforce, we believe in purpose intrinsically. It's in everything we do." The actual word *purpose* is rarely discussed at Salesforce, he said. "Instead, we spend considerable time up front aligning behind our core values of trust, customer success, innovation, and equality. These values shape every decision we make as a company, as teams, and as individuals."

As with a lot companies in our research at Go Forward to Work (GFTW) Institute, the intimate connection between Salesforce's purpose and its employees revealed the power of purpose to achieve fast results in 2020. From the start of the pandemic, Salesforce quickly stepped up to help governments in Rhode Island and New York City set up Covid-19 testing processes. Before any company had perfected a Covid-19 vaccine,

Salesforce teams had already developed a Vaccine Cloud application for vaccine administration. The company also teamed up with a number of its corporate partners to help put out an entirely new product in record time: Work.com, a suite of services that includes a command center for return-to-work readiness, plus tools and resources for contact tracing, employee wellness, emergency response management, and special shift management tools designed to help companies coordinate scheduling among remote workers. With so many small businesses in particular struggling to survive the pandemic, Salesforce launched a wide range of free online resources for them under the banner of Salesforce Care.[1]

Companies like Salesforce, with a high level of employee engagement through a shared common purpose, were much better prepared than most other companies were to go on the wartime footing that the pandemic called for. The e-commerce company Etsy, like most online retailers, experienced a sudden surge of orders during the first months of the pandemic in 2020. Amid the chaos, however, the people at Etsy saw a singular opportunity to demonstrate the power of its company purpose: to "keep commerce human."

When the Centers for Disease Control and Prevention recommended that everyone wear cloth face masks in public to slow the spread of Covid-19, mask manufacturers all over the world struggled to keep up with demand. It took Etsy's leadership just a few days to step up and show off the nimbleness and ingenuity among its makers of handmade goods. In no time at all, Etsy planned and launched a mask-making campaign among the 2.8 million sellers it had in March 2020.

"We put out the call," said Etsy CEO Josh Silverman. "'Hey, if you have a sewing machine, please start making masks.'" Etsy teams created a step-by-step guide for crafting and marketing face masks, which included links to sewing patterns. The tech team retrained its search engines to avoid showing Halloween masks and cosmetic facial masks. Etsy offered direct phone support to its top seven hundred face-mask sellers and took pains to confirm their ability to produce and ship.

Etsy backed up its effort by providing mask sellers with free listing credits. It also waived $5 million in advertising fees, created a grace

High-Return Practices for Competing in the New World of Work

1. Team out to explore your organizational purpose.
2. Promote purpose ownership.
3. Set a purpose-driven course for radical adaptability.

period for sellers unable to pay their bills on time, and paused its service-level enforcement actions. Etsy made a pandemic survival guide for all its sellers and lobbied its US government contacts to ensure that any relief legislation included the solo business operators who make up the core of its seller community (97 percent of Etsy sellers work from home, and 81 percent of them are women).[2]

Within days, there were twenty thousand new Etsy sellers producing masks. Two weeks later, the number had jumped to sixty thousand. Etsy sold $133 million worth of masks in April 2020 and gained twelve million first-time buyers.[3]

Etsy's purpose, to "keep commerce human," propelled the speed and thoroughness of its response to the pandemic. Helping these modest home-based companies thrive is at the heart of Etsy's purpose. It's also how the company grows and makes money. The two objectives are aligned, because Etsy doesn't make money unless its sellers do.

For companies like Salesforce and Etsy to mobilize all their stakeholders inside and outside the organization, the companies' purpose needed to be owned and driven like a grassroots movement in those companies. It's a lesson Keith learned years ago from his good friend, the late Tony Hsieh, and that lesson has taken on new resonance for the new world of work, through conversations with GFTW Institute faculty members Susan Sobbott, formerly president of global commercial services with American Express, and Hubert Joly, the former CEO of Best Buy.

In the 1994 bestseller *Built to Last*, Jim Collins and Jerry Porras celebrated the kind of visionary company "that exists for a purpose beyond just making money, that stands the test of time by virtue of the ability to continually renew itself from within." They cited Johnson & Johnson, with its purpose to "alleviate pain and suffering," and Disney's purpose "to use our imagination to bring happiness to millions."[4] Having a strong, enduring purpose is how these and other great companies have survived through decades of shifting strategies and recurring disruption in their industries.

The importance of purpose has never been greater than today. The fast pivots and deft execution demanded by disruptive change are easier to handle when your workforce is engaged and inspired by their shared understanding of the company purpose. Change is happening so fast that there may be times when purpose is your company's single most reliable point of reference, your home port in a storm.

Make no mistake, every aspect of radical adaptability requires shifts in behavior and attitudes that will provoke doubts within the organization as to *why*? Why change? Why *these* changes? Why now? Why bother? Without a unifying higher purpose to serve as your *why*, each initiative toward radical adaptability runs the risk of drowning in the daily tide of habit and inertia.

On the other hand, if you are able to activate your company's purpose as a *movement* among all its stakeholders, your purpose can function as a force multiplier for radical adaptability. Purpose can serve as a filter for priorities and decision-making, a glue that binds the organization's parts closer together, and a magnet for recruiting employees, acquiring new customers, and establishing new business partnerships. For companies that communicate an authentic purpose in a serious and consistent way, purpose has proven to be an engine of continuous transformative change.

The reason for this runs deep in human nature. We are inherently tribal creatures. We adapt to change fastest when we're motivated in cohesive groups by a shared purpose that provides us with a powerful *why*. When it comes to inspiring fundamental shifts in beliefs and behaviors, the organizations with unmatched records of success include Weight

Watchers, twelve-step programs, and religious groups. All of them rely on our innate need for tribal cohesion and belonging to guide people's behaviors toward an idealized, commonly valued purpose.

There was a time when having a shared mission was enough to drive organizational change. Employees could team out around their collective desire to be the biggest or the best. But missions are more about how. They're not about why. They're also limited by shifting market conditions. In the new world of work, change happens too fast for your mission to be a dependable unifying force. A new product from a well-funded startup can make your mission impossible tomorrow. Instead, you need a purpose that transcends marketplace uncertainties, one that transcends time itself. Your purpose should serve as the why that determines over the long term which new missions your company should pursue and which of your current missions are losing relevance and should be abandoned.

"Purpose is about having an impact beyond yourself, outside of the company's own profits," said Susan Sobbott. During her time at American Express, she reminded the people in her unit that their true purpose was to help small businesses succeed.

"I proposed that we could change the lives of millions of customers, and how those customers could change their communities and the economy, through our work together as a team," she recalled. "It was like turning on a switch. We started to see motivation and teamwork grow significantly because we had a higher purpose."

Susan's objective at the time was to achieve a 15 percent growth rate and a 20 percent reduction in costs. Those target numbers were vitally important, but management by objective lacks the power to motivate or spark innovation.

"To be honest," she said, "even I wasn't motivated by that." Instead, the inspirational intention of the unit's higher purpose, to change lives and communities, helped everyone remain mindful of what they were actually delivering for American Express customers. "That purpose led us to achieve the numbers," Susan concluded. "Our growth was the outcome, rather than the intent."

When leaders communicate the company purpose in this way, all achievement can be viewed through the lens of customer impact. Starbucks's purpose, for example, is "to inspire and nurture the human spirit." That purpose, which expresses a commitment to customer service beyond the company's immediate self-interest, has proven to be essential to its long-term profitability.

As the American Express example shows, the importance of purpose extends far beyond consumer product brand positioning. For any kind of organization, including business-to-business firms, purpose puts a premium on preserving long-term relationships—with customers, with vendors, with investors, with the entire outside world. Purpose can also serve as a guiding light to protect your organization from making short-term moves that might threaten those relationships.

Susan Sobbott faced one such threat during the 2008 financial crisis. When some of American Express's seven million small-business customers began falling behind on their payments, the company responded by reducing customer credit limits across the board, even for their best customers with excellent payment histories.

Customers reacted with a sense of betrayal and rage. "For years, we'd told them 'membership has its privileges,' and they believed us," Susan recalled. "Now, because of our own fear, we were viewing our customers as the enemy. We were depriving them of credit when they needed it the most."

Susan led the charge inside the company to undo the damage. "I had to go back to our purpose, and ask, how could we live up to our intent to help businesses thrive?" she said. "We had to think about the customers, not ourselves, and find the joint interests of our customers, our employees, the company, and our shareholders."

Susan persuaded her colleagues to refine the company's computer models so that only the riskiest customers had their credit lines reduced. For those customers, an appeals process was instituted, and managers were empowered to work with customers to make exceptions where possible. For other customers who were unable to pay on time, the team developed systems for modified payment schedules and reduced fees.

Led by its purpose of "helping small business do more business," American Express innovated by empowering its employees. Small business customers repaid American Express with their loyalty. Susan noted that American Express was the first in its industry to recover from the 2008 credit crisis and return to growth, having suffered the lowest levels of losses among all its competitors.

"We needed to think past our survival and think about the legacy of the American Express brand," she explained. "We were able to join interests with our customers and move forward with our purpose helping us look to the long term. Our customers trusted that we had their best interests in mind and we needed to live up to that promise to retain their loyalty."

People need to make a direct emotional connection with the company's purpose if that purpose is to inspire change. Unfortunately, few companies recognize this need, and that's why so many workplace change movements fail. The change is announced, people don't connect with it, they see others ignoring it, and apathy sets in. Radical adaptability is unlikely to land solidly within the leadership ranks and beyond unless people personally *feel* the purpose behind each of the methodologies we've described.

Purpose is how all of radical adaptability's high-return practices meet their ultimate expression and fulfillment. The secret to fully implementing radical adaptability is to involve people on your teams and throughout the organization in supercharging the company's purpose. That could mean that you either renew your vision of the company's existing purpose or explore a new statement of purpose. This chapter describes the high-return practices for supercharging your purpose through the three steps of teaming out to explore your purpose, promoting the personal ownership of purpose within every team member, and, finally, setting a purpose-driven long-term course for radical adaptability.

All along the way, the process of supercharging the company purpose will reveal which of your team members connect most profoundly with the changes that purpose inspires. If you can recognize these team members early on and support them appropriately, they will prove to be your champions for radical adaptability. From collaboration and agility through to business model innovation and workforce redesign, these people will be your company's most reliable agents of change in the new world of work.

Team Out to Explore Your Organizational Purpose

You can rely on all the high-return practices for collaboration, including teaming out, crowdsourcing, and collaborative problem-solving (CPS) to ensure that your company purpose is supercharged and cocreated by as many of the company's stakeholders as possible. For one thing, the process will give all of them a bigger stake in the outcome and a deeper investment in the change the new purpose represents. Another chief benefit of teaming out to supercharge your purpose is that the process reveals the stakeholders most excited and engaged by the new direction. Those are people you will need to count on as the company's vanguard for radically adaptable change.

Salim Ismail, author of *Exponential Organizations*, says that a lone startup founder can begin to attract like-minded investors and employees by declaring the startup's MTP, the massive transformative purpose that will define the startup's future course.[5] Established companies of all sizes can tap into the same source of inspirational power, he says, by extrapolating a purpose statement from the company's existing mission. The consumer products giant Unilever is now guided by a higher purpose that would have been unimaginable at its founding in 1929: "to make sustainable living commonplace."

It's a matter of identifying the why behind your how. Microsoft's shift in its purpose is a good illustration. The company's original purpose, declared by Bill Gates, had always been "a PC on every desk and in every home, running Microsoft software." In 2014, when Satya Nadella became CEO, he set Microsoft on a much more inspiring and enduring purpose: "to empower every person and every organization on the planet to achieve more." This purpose, because it's not limited by product categories or market conditions, has helped Microsoft focus its ongoing transformation.

In May 2016, Microsoft abandoned its mobile phone business and wrote off its entire $7 billion investment in this category. One month later, Microsoft purchased LinkedIn for $26.2 billion. For Microsoft's hundreds of thousands of employees, partners, and other stakeholders, both moves were completely understandable and aligned with Microsoft's explicit purpose "to empower people." For years, Microsoft hadn't empowered anyone in the mobile phone business, where it had long been a niche player with limited prospects for future growth and profit. On the other hand, integrating LinkedIn's massive user base with Microsoft's suite of software tools could be very empowering to many millions of people—and potentially very profitable.

If your company already has a well-known purpose statement, consider how supercharging its meaning could make it an authentic driver of change. Susan Sobbott recommends you start the process by assessing how the company lives out its purpose. Is it obvious in all the actions taken by leaders and in policies, processes, and plans? Use CPS to explore how well the statement is directing and motivating innovation. Can everyone in the company recite it? Are they clear about the values and principles that underlie it? Can they say how decisions are made with respect to those values and principles?

You'll find some clues to the answers all throughout the high-return practices of radical adaptability. How is the company's purpose expressed through the current culture of collaboration and inclusion? Through agility? Through support for employee resilience? Is the purpose present in your approaches to foresight? What about business innovation and workforce development? Are your strategies in these areas driven by a long-term vision, or are they more tactical and provisional? Purpose should be essential to your efforts at foresight. If your company purpose is detached from your strategic choices, how can all the company's teams pull together toward the future?

In the attempt to supercharge your higher purpose, you are likely to find the lowest-hanging fruit among your activities in philanthropy, sustainability, community, and diversity. These are the areas where you're already expected to think and act beyond immediate concerns for profit. Note which activities inspire the highest levels of energy, achievement, and passion within the organization. What are the common themes revealed by these activities? If they generate high levels of employee engagement, they might point in the direction of your company's authentic purpose.

This approach toward defining purpose is especially useful for B2B companies, which don't draw purpose from consumer brand identities in the way of Johnson & Johnson, Disney, and Microsoft. For example, North America's largest roofing manufacturer, GAF, has this purpose: "We protect what matters most." The company demonstrates its purpose by donating materials, time, and expertise in disaster recovery zones and in communities where GAF has plant facilities.

"You're finding your humanity in this process," said Susan Sobbott. "Once you discover how you are already impacting the people in your world, the path becomes clearer toward translating those actions into your purpose." She recommends a thought experiment not unlike the premise of the movie *It's a Wonderful Life*: try to imagine what the world would be like if your company didn't exist. That void left by your company's absence roughly reflects the shape of your company's true purpose. According to Susan, "Who you are on your best day, when you are most proud of your efforts, is a pretty clear path to your 'why.' That's because your emotional connection and pride comes from impact more than numbers."

Through crowdsourcing and CPS, you can engage your employees and all other stakeholders in these questions. If you have a purpose statement, do they understand it? If you don't have a purpose statement, ask them what makes them feel proudest about the company. Susan recommends polling your team. What do they love to tell family and friends about the company? When do they think the company is at its best? What do they wish it did more of? Ask what they feel most passionate about in their lives, both at work and beyond. Involve all the people who know your company the best: your employees, your customers, your vendors, your suppliers—all your stakeholders. Bring them all into the process early because they will inevitably become emissaries of your purpose in the future.

Through CPS, also ask employees about what they hear from customers. How do we make our customers feel? How are we making a difference in their lives, their businesses, and their communities? These are important questions. If many of your employees have trouble imagining what difference they're making in the lives of others, that's both a problem and an opportunity. Most people have trouble succeeding in jobs that lack a sense of meaning and purpose. If your company has been doing fine without a purpose, then finding one might produce a quantum leap in employee engagement and productivity.

Go directly to your customers. Susan recommends identifying about twenty of your ideal customers and asking them similar questions. You might gather groups of them together for CPS exercises. Ask what difference your company makes for them. What would they say might be your company purpose? Why do they prefer you to other companies? What would they do if your company didn't exist? Take these same questions to everyone you consider your important stakeholders, including strategic partners, vendors, suppliers, beneficiaries of your corporate philanthropy, and community members in places where you have operations.

By using CPS and breakout rooms in these ways, you can aggregate the thoughts and feelings of all your stakeholders. Areas of commonality will inevitably arise. Can you see a general consensus about how your company is most impactful on the lives of others? What about the areas where your company stirs the greatest passion and loyalty? Is there any activity in which your company is deemed essential and irreplaceable? Next, explore how these observations align with your financial results. Are you earning your revenue from the products and services that stir the greatest passions? Could these most passion-inspiring categories be the source of your company's niche appeal and competitive advantage?

Consider how Etsy's commitment to handcrafted goods is what distinguishes it from even the largest ecommerce retailers. The purpose of "keeping commerce human" is much more than an attractive notion that makes employees feel good about their jobs. Etsy's purpose is the source of its enduring competitive advantage. As long as Etsy's leadership commits wholeheartedly to keeping commerce human, it will continue to dominate its multibillion-dollar e-commerce niche. By keeping revenues and purpose in alignment, Etsy's healthy bottom line will be one of many positive outcomes from the pursuit of a higher purpose.

Promote Purpose Ownership

Identifying an organizational purpose takes time. When GFTW Institute faculty member Hubert Joly was leading the turnaround of Best Buy in the 2010s, it took the company two years to arrive at the right formulation for what Best Buy came to regard as its noble purpose: "To enrich our customers' lives through technology."[6]

Hubert says this purpose statement was designed to keep stretching Best Buy to be the best possible version of itself in perpetuity. "Twenty years from now," he writes in his book, *The Heart of Business*, "enriching the lives of customers through technology will still be relevant—even if TVs and personal computers no longer are."[7]

The first challenge posed by a new purpose statement of this kind is how to make it a concrete and meaningful reality for all your stakeholders. How can the company manifest its purpose? How can purpose be expressed and demonstrated in action, so that all stakeholders can recognize the nature of the change and pull together and cocreate with genuine tribal passion?

In the case of Best Buy, the top leadership puzzled over how its hundred thousand store associates could get Best Buy customers to connect with the company's purpose. How would all these associates need to behave so that Best Buy's new promise to enrich customers' lives really landed with them?

"If Best Buy were a person, how would she or he behave?" Hubert recalls asking. "What do we look like when we are at our best?" The company ran a series workshops in 2017 with store managers and others in management who had close contact with customers. Over time, they arrived at the idea that customers would want their Best Buy associate to be a kind of "inspiring friend," someone who knew more about technology than they did and would help them understand what would best fit their needs and budget.

How do you train store associates to deliver that message? You don't. You can't. For change of this kind to take root and grow, people need to feel personally inspired. Each of them needs to feel challenged to find personal meaning in the change. That's what will motivate them to co-elevate with their team members to go higher together and raise their game collectively, each for their own deeply felt reasons.

At 7:30 a.m. on a Saturday in 2017, Best Buy staff in stores all across the United States convened for two hours to discuss what kinds of behaviors would deliver the "inspired friend" feeling to customers. This was not a sales training with scripted lines and value propositions. Instead, store associates were asked to discuss what friendship meant to them: "Which of your friends do you admire most? What about those friends inspires you? That's the kind of inspiration you want to give our customers."

Hubert himself attended one of the training sessions in New York City and spoke about why he admired his older brother's energy and generosity. He sat and listened as one of the store associates told her story of being temporarily homeless after breaking up with an abusive boyfriend. Her coworkers at Best Buy helped her through this difficult time with kindness and care, and their friendship inspired her.

Everyone at Best Buy, including members of the company's board of directors, participated in these workshops and shared in this humble introspection about the true meaning of friendship. "Inspired friend" became the new expectation for behavior throughout the company. It was how Best Buy's purpose touched every working relationship in the organization. And when the company launched a spring 2018 marketing campaign, its new tagline, "Let's talk about what's possible," was built on encouraging customers to engage with Best Buy associates as inspired friends. The new campaign was Best Buy's invitation to visit its stores and engage with its people and its purpose.

Best Buy did a lot of things right to create this companywide change. Step by step, it turned the concept of an inspired friend into a movement throughout the organization. Because the inspired-friend idea was tied to the much larger purpose of enriching customer lives, Best Buy's new marketing campaign had the power to touch its associates' hearts. It focused their attention on the importance of being of service, of having empathy for those who know less than they do, and it subtly gave them a sense of status: "You are an inspiring friend to our customers. They are counting on you for your knowledge and expertise."

It's easy to forget that every individual at every level of an organization has a boundless appetite for personal fulfillment. As leaders, when we can tether the promise of personal fulfillment to the transformational changes needed by the organization, the sheer force of human nature will help accelerate the pace of change. Sustaining change as a movement requires leaders to show they care enough to participate themselves, sharing their own humble, fallible journeys too. Change needs to be a constant two-way dialogue on this open and vulnerable ground. When leaders show humility and actively demonstrate their pursuit of personal growth and change, they inspire their team members to become that much more open to confront their own challenges in the face of change.

When Ferrazzi Greenlight was involved in a huge transformative change project at GM, the regional president at the time participated directly in workshops not unlike the ones at Best Buy. He shared his personal journey with district sales managers, going as far as to offer what he believed he needed to focus on to become the leader he wanted to be to make the transformation possible. By displaying his vulnerability and humility to that community, he reinforced the point that everyone, from the top all the way down, was on this difficult journey of change together.

Successful change movements become self-sustaining when they encourage the team-building behaviors most directly connected to our tribal sense of belonging: service, candor, humility, and peer-to-peer commitment, to name just a few. Whenever change succeeds in unleashing new value, the value is realized at this level within the organization, amid the interpersonal relationships and interdependencies that set the tone of effective teamwork. These behaviors are notoriously the most difficult for leaders to influence. They are all but impossible to influence without personally engaging with purpose.

People are naturally suspicious of change. When mission-driven or sales-driven changes are introduced, people are often instructed to discard their familiar set of well-practiced behaviors and adopt new methods that are unfamiliar and may be unappealing. Even with financial incentives, tactical changes divorced from purpose are rarely able to sustain authentic employee engagement. It's one of many reasons why studies show that less than 30 percent of change actually sticks. Purpose-driven change, by contrast, never needs to disparage the old ways as being bad or wrong. Instead, it engages employees by connecting change to both the employees' own personal growth and career advancement.

Best Buy associates were introduced to the inspired-friend concept as a cause for celebration. The company was at the tail end of a long, difficult turnaround that had begun in 2012. The inspired-friend approach marked a new exciting chapter in Best Buy's history, one that promised ample opportunities for store associates to learn and grow, both personally and professionally.

Making people open to change is both a science and an art. It requires creating workplace environments that make change inviting, comfortable, and safe. In our work with GM's change effort, we recognized that the more authentic and open district managers were with each other, the deeper their bonds went. That was a sacred space we worked hard to protect. Participants constantly had open channels where they could report the sources of resistance and challenges that were preventing them from participating in the changes needed for transformation. They had a direct channel all the way up to leadership, and leadership was committed to making quick decisions and responding to people on the ground. When you invite people to share their struggles in this way, you must provide them with a psychologically safe environment where they can express themselves and know that they've been heard.

This last point is an important reminder that, as leaders, we are in the business of energy management. Amy Edmondson, the Harvard researcher who has done groundbreaking work on psychological safety, has studied the important role that purpose plays in generating the energy necessary for successful collaboration. She and her team have found that the while the trust generated by psychological safety is essential for collaboration, excellence is only achieved through the addition of a shared sense of purpose. In their equation, trust + purpose = energy. Wherever team energy is lacking, take the measure of mutual trust and shared purpose among team members. If there is slack in one or the other, the collaboration risks running out of fuel.[8]

Countless studies attest to how purpose is central to preventing burnout and to motivating employees to go the extra mile for a cause or an idea that is larger than themselves. When the going gets tough, purpose can be a storehouse of energy and resilience. For similar reasons, agility, with its focus on creating meaningful value for customers, is also highly dependent on purpose as its source of energy and drive. Recall David Frazee's cautionary note about agile work design at 3M. For agility to maintain team energy and reach peak productivity, assigned tasks must be small enough to be achievable but large enough to be *meaningful*.

Activating purpose throughout the organization has typically been more difficult for B2B companies. A 2019 survey of B2B executives by the Association of National Advertisers showed that 86 percent agreed that "purpose sets a clear 'North Star' for the business, articulating why it exists," but only 24 percent agreed that "purpose is embedded in [the] business. Purpose is activated across the business from culture and innovation to operations and engagement with society." Additionally, 56 percent of all respondents said that purpose "feels more like a PR exercise than authentic commitment."[9]

For all companies, but especially for B2B companies, purpose can provide a valuable path for teaming out with stakeholders outside the company—customers, vendors, suppliers, and other companies in adjacent industries. This kind of purpose-driven thinking is why Ferrazzi

Greenlight jumped into action in 2020 and launched the GFTW Institute. We looked to our purpose—team transformation—and saw how by teaming out through our clients and all their stakeholders, we could develop a central place for developing change agents in an environment of unprecedented change and uncertainty.

This same approach reflects how Salesforce has developed its outstanding reputation as a purpose-driven company. "The way we think about it," said Simon Mulcahy, "customer success is our second most important value after trust. This means our success comes from making end users successful and not so much from convincing buyers to buy. There is a big difference, because it means we're not just in the technology business. Our purpose includes education, enablement, and career development. It's why we've invested so much in customer communities and in Trailhead, our free learning platform."

That commitment is reflected in Salesforce's philanthropic efforts. When Salesforce announced the launch of its Education Cloud for K–12 students, CEO and founder Marc Benioff said, "A company like ours can't be successful in an unsuccessful economy or in an unsuccessful environment or where the school system doesn't work. We have to take responsibility for all of those things."[10]

A purpose-driven program that's aimed at benefiting the *customers of your customers* has the potential to go beyond mere marketing and become a powerful movement. In the fall of 2010, when the fallout from the global financial crisis had left the US economy in a recession, the small-business unit at American Express hatched a plan to drive holiday shoppers to independent retailers. Big retailers had Black Friday, and online retail had claimed Cyber Monday. So American Express launched Small Business Saturday. The company provided free Facebook and Twitter ads to its small-business customers and offered American Express shoppers $25 rebates when they shopped at small businesses.

The popularity of this relatively modest initial effort led American Express to aim bigger the following year. What started as a US initiative went global. Any small business could participate in Small Business Saturday, and American Express issued gift cards for shoppers who used other cards to make their purchases. The CEO of American Express was quoted as saying "I don't care if you use cash." Delta Air Lines, Google, and FedEx joined what was by then a movement, and FedEx distributed tens of thousands of $25 American Express gift cards to reward shoppers for patronizing small businesses.[11]

The Small Business Saturday project naturally drew a lot of attention to American Express and raised the company's standing in the eyes of its merchants. That, however, was just the outcome of a campaign with the higher purpose of "helping small business do more business." By generating a movement that went beyond American Express's immediate marketing goals, the company was able to attract contributions from powerful corporate partners and even from politicians. Big-city mayors participated in the annual Small Business Saturday launch in subsequent years, and at the start of the 2014 holiday shopping season, President Obama tweeted one morning: "As we mark #SmallBusiness-Saturday, let us continue to encourage the entrepreneurial spirit wherever we find it."[12]

Set a Purpose-Driven Course for Radical Adaptability

South Africa's largest health insurer is a company called Discovery. It was founded during the country's postapartheid era by two insurance actuaries who had the idea they could flip the purpose of health insurance. Instead of just paying for people's care when they got sick, why not offer health insurance with the added purpose of helping people stay well?

Discovery founder Adrian Gore knew that as much as 70 percent of health-care costs are driven by chronic illnesses brought on by poor lifestyle choices—overeating, smoking, lack of exercise. So Discovery launched an insurance product called Vitality Active Rewards, which gives policyholders incentives to earn rewards by working out (while logged on to their personal fitness devices), eating well, and losing weight.[13]

Discovery applies the science of behavioral economics to give policyholders immediate gratification for making healthy choices. Holders of the insurer's Vitality cards get 25 percent discounts on healthy food purchased at partnering grocers. Discovery will finance the purchase of your Apple watch and then send you immediate rewards (store credit for a coffee or a healthy smoothie) when the watch indicates you've finished working out. You also get the option of donating the value of your reward to charity. If you're active enough, Discovery will cut your monthly payments on the Apple watch all the way down to zero. A study of this *loss-framed* incentive proved it is exceptionally effective in helping extremely overweight people become more fit.[14]

Although Discovery's founders launched Vitality Active Rewards on the simple gut instinct that its purpose made sense, the company now has secured an enormous data set from almost four million policyholders, and this information proves the program's effectiveness. The data enables the company to fine-tune its incentives to maximize both company profitability and policyholder savings. The effectiveness of the program's purpose is also revealed in the data: policyholders enjoy measurably healthier lives.

They also live longer. In 2001, Discover added a life insurance product that provides similar incentives to live long and prosper. Discovery Life Insurance rapidly became South Africa's top provider, outselling competitors that had been in the business more than one hundred years. The massive data set is now such a durable competitive advantage for Discovery that other South African insurers haven't even attempted to copy its unique life insurance business model.

Discovery has since expanded its reach beyond its home country by partnering with insurers in the United States, China, and the United Kingdom, all of which run Vitality Active Rewards programs under their own brand names. Discovery's purpose-driven business model, founded on a hunch about human behavior, is now the centerpiece of a financial services holding company with more than $4 billion in annual revenue.[15] Discovery's proprietary health data is a sustainable source of competitive advantage because even if the insurance industry is disrupted in the future, Discovery's purpose, to improve human health, will endure. Every day that Discovery's policyholders provide new data to enrich the company's database, Discovery gets smarter about what it takes to encourage healthy human behavior—knowledge that will always be extremely valuable, no matter how it's deployed.

When your company's future is tied to its purpose, your sights can be raised above the everyday competitive fray. In the case of Discovery, purpose helped the company's founders recognize that they could make better lives for customers and make more money at the same time by encouraging its policyholders to stay well.

At Best Buy, Hubert Joly put the company's purpose at the center of its business innovation approach. "It fundamentally changed our strategy and how we did business," he said. The company performed months of intense data analysis to identify new areas of opportunity—a business innovation process driven by purpose. Best Buy zoomed in on industries involved with key human needs—security, health and wellness, food, entertainment, and communications—and asked, "Where can we enrich lives through technology?" How could the company diversify beyond its retail model and into business models that build lasting customer relationships through technology solutions?

In 2019, the company launched a new unit called Best Buy Health, which aims to bring personal and home health technologies to market. For a global population with increasing life spans, Best Buy Health foresees the unit providing remote monitoring tools and care coordination services as benefits in health insurance plans.

The new unit passed what Hubert calls the four-question test:

- Does it fit with our purpose as a company?

- Is it good for the customer?

- Can we deliver?

- *And* can we make money?[16]

Notice the order of the questions. It helps define a purpose-driven company. Business ideas that don't fit the company purpose are not worth pursuing to the next question. That's mainly because when you use purpose to drive business innovation in this way, you open up many more possibilities than you could imagine.

If Hubert had not made this explicit link between purpose and strategy, his team never would have recognized many other business opportunities. The purpose of "enriching lives through technology" prompted the Best Buy repair operation, Geek Squad, to expand its offering and provide help for all kinds tech problems, not just tech bought at Best Buy. The company developed teams of in-home advisers to provide home entertainment solutions best designed on site, not in the store—because isn't that what an inspired friend would do?

The ultimate value of purpose is that it directly supports the perpetual evolution of the organization as a radically adaptable organism. The vision of a company *built to last*, to borrow a term from Jim Collins, is one that grows along a purpose-guided path into the uncertain future, with products, services, and profits as outcomes of its progress toward its ultimate purpose.

Back in 2018, Larry Fink, CEO of BlackRock, the world's largest asset manager, shook the investment world with his annual letter to CEOs. Titled "A Sense of Purpose," the letter called on CEOs of companies desiring BlackRock investment to articulate a clear company purpose behind their strategies. "Without a sense of purpose, no company, either public or private, can achieve its full potential," he wrote. Without a long-term focus, companies "will succumb to short-term pressures to distribute earnings, and, in the process, sacrifice investments in employee development, innovation, and capital expenditures that are necessary for long-term growth." Since then, he has cautioned CEOs that BlackRock considers companies without credible plans for carbon-neutral futures not attractive investments: "Climate risk is investment risk."[17]

Earlier, we cited the case of GM's transformation to a carbon-neutral vehicle fleet. All over the world, companies are using purpose to make the transition to a new future of energy that their company founders would not recognize. The former Norwegian state oil company, now called Equinor, announced that 49 percent of its annual 2020 earnings had come from renewable energy investments.[18] Under its purpose "to turn natural resources into energy for people, and progress for society," Equinor has divested of holdings in gas stations and shale oil drilling and has partnered with BP (formerly British Petroleum) to build a massive offshore wind project in Brooklyn, New York, as a staging area for wind projects up and down the US East Coast.[19]

BP, notorious for the disastrous 2010 Deepwater Horizon oil spill in the Gulf of Mexico, has since embraced a new purpose of "reimagining energy for people and our planet." The purpose underpins the company's long-term strategy of reducing oil and gas production by 40 percent, halting exploration in new countries, and developing electric car charging facilities. It filed applications in several major US states to become a supplier of renewable power to consumers under a new subsidiary, BP Energy Retail.

The transformations of such enormous capital-intensive companies is unprecedented. It's as if the old New York Central Railroad back in the 1950s had expanded into the airline business with New York Central Air or had used its position in the diesel fuel market to launch a network of New York Central filling stations. Any of the old US railroads, if they had embraced a purpose such as "keeping America moving," could have leveraged their brand reputations for service excellence by offering travelers interconnected ecosystems of transport services. The railroads could have transformed their train stations into hubs for connections to airports and highways. Instead, they stayed on track with their original missions, and rolled their way into mergers, bankruptcies and oblivion.

Ironically, when we fast-forward to 2021, we see how GM's purpose has led it into the railroad business! Having invested billions toward making vehicles that won't require the burning of fossil fuels, GM has become a leader in the hydrogen fuel cell and battery technologies required for all forms of clean-running transportation. As a result, GM is partnering and sharing its know-how with the locomotive maker Wabtec Corporation and the heavy-truck company Navistar.[20] By replacing GM's famed internal-combustion engines with a new commitment to proprietary battery and propulsion technologies, GM has opened up an endless array of new licensing and partnership opportunities in the areas of carbon-free, climate-friendly transportation and energy storage.

GM is so much more than a carmaker today, and there's no telling what a purpose-driven GM will look like in the years to come. To embrace total uncertainty of this kind as a source of unbounded opportunity is what it means to be truly radically adaptable. And this ability is without a doubt what separates the best from the rest in the new world of work.

GUIDING QUESTIONS
How to Compete in the New World of Work

Does our company rally around a sufficiently aspirational and well-articulated purpose that guides and inspires all stakeholders?

> Companies that articulate a meaningful and authentic purpose will lead in attracting talent and investment and are more resilient in the face of adversity. A company's purpose must look beyond the mission of increasing market share and focuses on macro-level changes that distinguish the company from the products or services it sells.

Does our company's purpose guide our innovation and future-proofing strategy?

> At radically adaptable companies, their purpose is a key driver of corporate strategy and innovation initiatives and not just a stand-alone aspiration. A company's purpose defines the products and services the company offers and helps leadership stay true to core values, even as markets and circumstances force shifts in demand.

Futurelogue

I magine that the clock is ticking down toward midnight and the arrival of a new year, ten years from now. You are looking back on a decade that was unlike any other in human history. Technologies, business models, and workforce styles have all changed in unpredictable ways and much faster than almost anyone had foreseen. For some, it has been a decade of unimaginable challenges and opportunities. For others, it has been a decade of turmoil, decline, and disaster.

Happy New Year! Take a moment to ask your future self, ten years from now, what you could have done better to prepare. What choices did you make in those ten years—for yourself, for your teams, for your businesses—to stay competitive in the emerging new world of work? Did you apply the lessons of this book? Did you engage with our proven high-return practices? Did you co-elevate and team out to bring others along with you?

Or, when things got tough, did you revert to the old ways that you knew best? Did you and your organization adapt to change only grudgingly? Or did you practice radical adaptability proactively, in the spirit of catapulting your career and your organization forward? Your ability to remain radically adaptable through the unpredictable years ahead may be one of the only things you can count on.

Start anywhere. As you use this book and try out its high-return practices, you'll discover that the elements of radical adaptability function as a virtuous loop, each element uplifting the effectiveness of all the others. You have the opportunity to start today, to be an agent of change, to lead your teams in constant reinvention through the seven elements of radical adaptability.

Consider how Indeed, the world's largest job search and hiring website, has already employed radical adaptability to thrive in the new world of work. Based in Austin, Texas, Indeed was founded in 2004 and has been profitable since 2007. At the start of 2020, it had been growing by 40 percent annually for five years running. The second quarter of 2020, during the economic slowdown caused by the pandemic, was the company's first down quarter *ever*, but Indeed recovered quickly and its 2020 revenues matched its 2019 results. That swift rebound was a direct consequence of years of practicing the key leadership competencies of collaboration, agility, resilience, and foresight at every level of the organization. Together these elements have created a reinforcement loop that powers Indeed's business model innovation and workforce flexibility, all in service of its strong corporate purpose.

Indeed was a small technology firm with about five hundred employees when it was acquired in 2012 by Recruit Group, a Japanese conglomerate. The following year, Recruit Group senior executive Hisayuki "Deko" Idekoba stepped in as Indeed CEO. He brought with him the parent company's exceptional culture of corporate foresight, in which "midrange" strategic planning has a seven- to ten-year time horizon. Deko's leadership team instituted regular scenario planning as a tool for anticipating change within economic cycles. At the start of 2020, Indeed's leadership had already expected a slowdown in the economic cycle for several years and had developed detailed scenario plans for how to react.

"Thanks to Deko and our relationship with Recruit Group, scenario planning became a muscle that the entire leadership team developed extensively," said Chris Hyams, Indeed's current CEO. "We were able to do really long-term thinking, and this gave us a huge advantage in the early days of the pandemic."

In the spring of 2020, when the pandemic had thrown twenty-five million Americans out of work, certain sectors of the economy nonetheless experienced dire labor shortages. The health-care and grocery industries faced extreme demand for essential workers. Major retailers with global operations were inundated by orders from online shoppers. They all needed to onboard new talent virtually overnight. But how do you onboard five thousand new employees *right now,* when your organization is used to onboarding a thousand people in three months and your recruiting team is the same size as before? How do you even screen so many applicants?

That's where Indeed saw the opportunity to leverage its corporate purpose to help its clients on a much deeper level. Indeed is a profoundly purpose-driven company. Everyone at the firm—from receptionists to software engineers to salespeople to the CEO—can tell you how they contribute to Indeed's purpose: "We help people get jobs."

Indeed already had a strategic goal of getting "closer to the hire." In its most basic form, job-hunting is a four-step process: search, apply, interview, hire. To get closer to that last step of hiring, Indeed needed to do a huge amount of intermediary work to make the first three steps move faster and easier. That's no small undertaking for a platform like Indeed, which hosts more than one billion job applications per year. In this transformation, the company's leadership applied each element of radical adaptability.

First, Indeed aligned its purpose with customer needs and reached out to every major employer that was hiring essential workers—whether they had ever been an Indeed customer or not—and offered to help them for *free.* Concurrently, its customer success teams called clients and advised them to pause their monthly subscriptions if they weren't currently hiring. Why pay for something if you're not getting value from it? It might seem counterintuitive to give away your product for free or to encourage your existing clients to cancel sales, but that's exactly what Indeed did *because* one of Indeed's core values is that clients pay for performance. And by giving away its services for free to organizations in need, Indeed engendered tremendous customer goodwill.

Second, the leadership team tasked the company's internal product accelerator team to tear down the entire client recruiting process and deploy agile thinking to rebuild it as a simpler and faster process. (The accelerator is an incubator program that allows employees to pitch new business ideas to the executive team, which uses a virtual venture-capital investing model to fund accelerator projects.) Within four weeks, the accelerator team developed a new highly automated service that gathered candidate résumés, screened them, automatically scheduled interviews, and, for some clients, even made employment offers. Indeed then used this service to help a major European health-care provider hire more than sixty-five thousand new employees in six months—an unimaginable result with traditional approaches to recruiting.

Third, Indeed innovated through its business product portfolio. The company rapidly created a new video-interviewing platform that answered the urgent need of employers to conduct safe and convenient job interviews. Indeed's leaders wanted to give job seekers a seamless digital experience so they could apply and interview for jobs with just a few button clicks. The leaders also wanted to automate workflows and eliminate 80 percent of their clients' recruiting time spent on manual and administrative tasks. After testing this video prototype with a few clients, Indeed invited twenty-five hundred clients to participate in a "Virtual Hiring Tour across America." Indeed provided $20 million in free advertising to attract job seekers to the tour, which resulted in ninety thousand interviews and twenty thousand hires. All virtual!

Fourth, Indeed leveraged collaboration through inclusion and co-elevation to build a resilient company culture in a year filled with public health emergencies, social justice protests, and economic uncertainty. On March 4, 2020, the day after Indeed had sent home every one of its 10,000 workers, it held its first entirely virtual all-company meeting. The meeting's most voted-on issue concerned the suddenly unemployed 250-person catering staff at the now-empty Austin headquarters. Indeed's leadership responded by committing to support the catering staff throughout the pandemic, even though they were contract workers and not technically Indeed employees.

During periods of social unrest in 2020, the company's employee-led Inclusion Resource Groups became profoundly valuable forums through which Indeed employees in Europe and Asia could also join in the conversation about racial justice in America. "The Inclusion Resource Groups became the glue that held the entire company culture together when everyone was remote," said Chris Hyams. Noting that the groups were formed in 2016, he added, "This was only possible because we had a solid foundation and infrastructure for inclusion and collaboration before the pandemic hit."

And finally, Indeed evolved its own workforce strategy to compete in this new world of work. To build a resilient workforce, Indeed pixelated its work roles and attempts to accommodate each employee's preferences for work full-time in office, full-time remote, or some hybrid combination of the two. Chris is quick to note that this is just the start of a continuous process of adjustment. Unlike most startups, Indeed was founded in two locations—in Austin, Texas, and Stamford, Connecticut. "We have the humility and experience of having run a hybrid business since our early days to know that it's really hard," Chris said. "We have an initial conviction, and we're going to test and measure and recalibrate into the future as needed." Experimentation, measuring results, and recalibrating are essential to every element of radical adaptability.

Indeed's practice of foresight set everything in motion for its response to the new world of work. Each quarter, the leadership team would select several topics and run half-day scenario planning exercises around them: "What would Indeed look like if it were ten times larger? How would this increased size impact revenue planning, future product innovation, and customer segmentation? How would it impact our response to an economic downturn?" These kinds of questions helped provide the team with a framework to align around strategy, identify early warning signals, and plan for new opportunities. This regular practice of foresight, which prepared the company for the tumult of 2020, is what will help the company see around corners in the decades to come.

Now is the time for you to start down this path. As a team leader and a change agent in your company, it's up to you to step into the arena and make these kinds of choices to catapult your career and your business forward.

Disrupt or be disrupted. We are all at a crossroads. For that reason, we hope that you will spread the leadership elements of these high-return practices beyond the four corners of your company—to non-profits you volunteer with and to the governments you elect. Every community can benefit by practicing radical adaptability. We have a collective responsibility to help shepherd other organizations in society to fast-forward to the future. To lead, and not react. To inspire abundance for all, and not for a select few. To include, and not divide.

The next decade will offer endless new possibilities for prosperity, but only if we stop speculating about the future of work and become evangelists for learning, growing, and adapting together. At the GFTW Institute, we'll continue to research and develop the high-return practices of radical adaptability. We invite you to join us in this movement. Become a member of our faculty. Help us build a global network of change agents. This journey has just started, and there is so much more to learn. Together we will cocreate the models of success in this new world of work.

Notes

Chapter 1

1. Danger Ranger, "Remembering Larry: A Man for Our Time," *Burning Man Journal*, April 18, 2019, https://journal.burningman.org/2019/04/opinion/serious-stuff/remembering-larry-a-man-for-our-time.

2. Burning Man, "Event FAQ," https://burningman.org/event/preparation/faq/#qwhatisburningman, accessed July 22, 2021.

3. Lara Richards, "All of London's Michelin-Star Restaurants Doing Takeaway and Delivery," *TimeOut*, January 29, 2021, www.timeout.com/london/news/all-of-londons-michelin-star-restaurants-doing-takeaway-and-delivery-012921.

4. Sarah Drumm, "How to Pivot Properly," *Raconteur*, October 27, 2020, www.raconteur.net/business-strategy/risk/pandemic-pivot.

5. Ibid.

6. Alfred Chua, "China Airlines Eyes Continued Growth in Profitable Cargo Market," *Flight Global*, April 8, 2021, www.flightglobal.com/airlines/china-airlines-eyes-continued-growth-in-profitable-cargo-market/143215.article.

7. John Rettie, "The Art Cars and Mutant Vehicles of Burning Man 2019," *Motortrend*, September 11, 2019, www.motortrend.com/features/art-cars-mutant-vehicles-burning-man-2019.

8. "Award for Tsunami Warning Pupil," BBC News, September 9, 2005, http://news.bbc.co.uk/2/hi/uk_news/4229392.stm.

9. Ned Rozell, "1946 Tsunami Survivor Shares Her Story," Alaska Science Forum, University of Alaska, Fairbanks, Geophysical Institute, December 31, 2014, https://www.gi.alaska.edu/alaska-science-forum/1946-tsunami-survivor-shares-her-story.

10. Florin Diacu, *Megadisasters: The Science of Predicting the Next Catastrophe* (Princeton, NJ: Princeton University Press, 2010).

11. "Award for Tsunami Warning Pupil."

12. Ibid.

Chapter 2

1. Keith Ferrazzi, "How Virtual Teams Can Outperform Traditional Teams," hbr.org, September 26, 2012, https://hbr.org/webinar/2012/10/how -virtual-teams-can-outperfo-2.

2. Karen Sobel-Lojeski, "The Subtle Ways Our Screens Are Pushing Us Apart," hbr.org, April 8, 2015, https://hbr.org/2015/04/the-subtle-ways-our -screens-are-pushing-us-apart.

3. "What Happens at an Amish Barn Raising?," *Amish America*, https:// amishamerica.com/what-happens-at-an-Amish-barn-raising, accessed July 22, 2021.

4. Amy C. Edmondson, *The Fearless Organization: Creating Psychological Safety in the Workplace for Learning, Innovation, and Growth* (New York: John Wiley & Sons, 2018).

5. GitLab, "Asynchronous Collaboration," in "How Do You Collaborate and Whiteboard Remotely?" https://about.gitlab.com/company/culture/all -remote/collaboration-and-whiteboarding/#asynchronous-collaboration, accessed July 22, 2021; Dropbox, "What Is Asynchronous Communication?" https://experience.dropbox.com/resources/asynchronous-communication, accessed July 22, 2021.

6. Brené Brown, "The Power of Vulnerability," filmed June 2010, TEDxHouston, video, 20:03, https://www.ted.com/talks/brene_brown_the _power_of_vulnerability?language=en. This TEDx talk has been viewed more than 52 million times.

7. Arvind Malhotra, Ann Majchrzak, Lâle Kesebi, and Sean Looram, "Developing Innovative Solutions through Internal Crowdsourcing," *MIT Sloan Management Review*, summer 2017, https://sloanreview.mit.edu/article /developing-innovative-solutions-through-internal-crowdsourcing.

Chapter 3

1. Keith Ferrazzi with Noel Weyrich, *Leading Without Authority: How the New Power of Co-Elevation Can Break Down Silos, Transform Teams, and Reinvent Collaboration* (New York: Currency, 2020).

2. John W. Tukey, "The Future of Data Analysis," *Annals of Mathematical Statistics* 33, no. 1 (March 1962): 1–67.

3. Ron Carucci, " Executives Fail to Execute Strategy Because They're Too Internally Focused," hbr.org, November 13, 2017, https://hbr.org/2017 /11/executives-fail-to-execute-strategy-because-theyre-too-internally -focused; Bridges Business Consultancy Int., "20-Year Results from Survey- ing Strategy Implementation," http://www.bridgesconsultancy.com/wp

-content/uploads/2016/10/20-Years-of-Strategy-Implementation-Research-2
.pdf.

4. Fred Wilson, "Why Early Stage Venture Investments Fail," usv.com,
November 30, 2007, https://www.usv.com/writing/2007/11/why-early-stage
-venture-investments-fail/.

5. Richard Nieva, "YouTube Started as an Online Dating Site," cnet.com,
March 14, 2016, https://www.cnet.com/news/youtube-started-as-an-online
-dating-site/.

6. Darrell Rigby, Sarah Elk, and Steve Berez, *Doing Agile Right: Transformation without Chaos* (Boston: Harvard Business Review Press, 2020).

Chapter 4

1. Larry Dignan, "Apple's Q4: Mac, iPad, Apple Watch Sales, Services
Shine Ahead of iPhone 12 Sales," *Between the Lines* (blog), ZDNet, October 29, 2020, www.zdnet.com/article/apples-q4-mac-ipad-apple-watch-sales
-services-shine.

2. American Psychological Association, "Building Your Resilience,"
2012, www.apa.org/topics/resilience.

3. Mary Baker, "Gartner Survey Reveals 82% of Company Leaders Plan
to Allow Employees to Work Remotely Some of the Time," Gartner, press
release, July 14, 2020, www.gartner.com/en/newsroom/press-releases/2020
-07-14-gartner-survey-reveals-82-percent-of-company-leaders-plan-to-allow
-employees-to-work-remotely-some-of-the-time.

4. World Health Organization, "Mental Health in the Workplace,"
WHO, www.who.int/teams/mental-health-and-substance-use/mental-health
-in-the-workplace, accessed July 22, 2021.

5. Matthew Gavidia, "How Has Covid-19 Affected Mental Health,
Severity of Stress among Employees?" *American Journal of Managed Care*,
April 20, 2020, www.ajmc.com/view/how-has-covid19-affected-mental
-health-severity-of-stress-among-employees.

Chapter 5

1. Jim Kouzes, "Looking Out the Window at the Future of Learning,"
ATD Links (blog), Association for Talent Development, September 28, 2010,
www.td.org/newsletters/atd-links/looking-out-the-window-at-the-future-of
-learning.

2. Paul Saffo, "Six Rules for Effective Forecasting," *Harvard Business
Review*, July–August 2007, https://hbr.org/2007/07/six-rules-for-effective
-forecasting.

3. University of Houston Foresight Department, "25% of Fortune 500 Practices Foresight," www.houstonforesight.org/25-of-fortune-500-practices-foresight, accessed July 22, 2021.

4. "Preparing for a Pandemic," *Harvard Business Review* (May 2006): 20–40, https://hbr.org/2006/05/preparing-for-a-pandemic.

5. Bill Gates, "The Next Outbreak? We're Not Ready," TED talk, 2015, transcript, www.ted.com/talks/bill_gates_the_next_outbreak_we_re_not_ready/transcript.

6. Leo Tilman, *Agility: How to Navigate the Unknown and Seize Opportunity in a World of Disruption* (Virginia: Missionday, 2019).

7. Ibid.

8. Eamon Tiernan, "Wimbledon Had Pandemic Insurance and Are Getting $226 Million," *7News*, April 9, 2020, https://7news.com.au/sport/wimbledon/wimbledon-had-pandemic-insurance-and-are-getting-getting-226-million-c-966783.

9. Tony Hsieh, *Delivering Happiness: A Path to Profits, Passion, and Purpose* (New York: Grand Central Publishing, 2013).

10. Angela Wilkinson and Roland Kupers, "Living in the Futures," *Harvard Business Review* (May 2013), https://hbr.org/2013/05/living-in-the-futures.

11. Damien McGuinness, "How a Cyber Attack Transformed Estonia," *BBC News*, April 27, 2017, www.bbc.com/news/39655415.

12. NATO Cooperative Cyber Defence Centre of Excellence, "Locked Shields," 2021, https://ccdcoe.org/exercises/locked-shields.

13. Amy Maxmen and Jeff Tollefson, "Two Decades of Pandemic War Games Failed to Account for Donald Trump," *Nature*, August 4, 2020, www.nature.com/articles/d41586-020-02277-6.

14. Adam Grant, "Building a Culture of Learning at Work," *Strategy+Business*, February 3, 2021, www.strategy-business.com/article/Building-a-culture-of-learning-at-work.

Chapter 6

1. Mary Barra, "General Motors Intends to Lead the Auto Industry and the World to a Net-Zero-Carbon Future," *Pulse* (blog), LinkedIn, January 28, 2021, www.linkedin.com/pulse/general-motors-intends-lead-auto-industry-world-future-mary-barra.

2. Chris Isidore, "GM Unveils Its Next 'Big' Electric Vehicle: The Tiny Bolt EUV," *CNN Business*, February 15, 2021, https://edition.cnn.com/2021/02/14/business/gm-chevrolet-bolt/index.html.

3. Barra, "General Motors Intends."

4. Theodore Levitt, "Marketing Myopia," *Harvard Business Review* 38 (1960): 45–56.

5. Brooke Henderson, "We're Eating a Lot More Pizza during the Pandemic; Why Domino's Is Getting the Biggest Slice of the Pie," *Fortune*, August 12, 2020, https://fortune.com/2020/08/12/coronavirus-food-trends -takeout-delivery-pizza-dominos-covid.

6. Rachel Pittman, "Domino's Fights Delivery Driver Shortage with Robots," *QSR Magazine*, October 24, 2019, www.qsrmagazine.com /exclusives/domino-s-fights-delivery-driver-shortage-robots.

7. "The Future of Delivery Is Self-Driving," Domino's, https:// selfdrivingdelivery.dominos.com/en, accessed July 22, 2021.

8. Research and Markets, "$34 Billion Delivery Robots Market—Global Forecast 2024: Reduction in Delivery Costs in Last-Mile Deliveries Driving Growth," Intrado Globe Newswire, February 14, 2019, www.globenewswire .com/news-release/2019/02/14/1725475/0/en/34-Billion-Delivery-Robots -Market-Global-Forecast-2024-Reduction-in-Delivery-Costs-in-Last-Mile -Deliveries-Driving-Growth.html.

9. American Sleep Apnea Association, "Sleep Apnea Information for Clinicians," www.sleepapnea.org/learn/sleep-apnea-information-clinicians, accessed July 22, 2021.

10. Larry Keeley, *Ten Types of Innovation: The Discipline of Building Break-throughs* (Hoboken, NJ: John Wiley & Sons, 2013).

11. August Brown, "Black Creatives Helped Turn Clubhouse into the Next Tech Unicorn. But Who Stands to Gain?" *Los Angeles Times*, February 1, 2021, www.latimes.com/entertainment-arts/music/story/2021-02-01 /clubhouse-app-hip-hop-black-creatives-billion-valuation.

Chapter 7

1. See Anthem's "Our Company" page at www.anthemcorporate responsibility.com/our-company, accessed July 22, 2021.

2. Clayton Christensen Institute, "Jobs to Be Done," www.christensen institute.org/jobs-to-be-done, accessed July 22, 2021.

3. Robert S. Duboff, *Market Research Matters: Tools and Techniques for Aligning Your Business* (New York: John Wiley & Sons, 2000).

Chapter 8

1. Salesforce, "Salesforce Care: Supporting Small Businesses through Covid-19 Recovery," *News & Insights* (blog), Salesforce, April 8, 2020,

www.salesforce.com/news/stories/salesforce-care-supporting-small-businesses
-through-covid-19-recovery.

2. Etsy.

3. Etsy.

4. James C. Collins, *Built to Last*, 3rd ed. (New York: HarperBusiness, 2002).

5. Salim Ismail, *Exponential Organizations: Why New Organizations Are Ten Times Better, Faster, and Cheaper Than Yours (and What to Do About It)* (New York: Diversion Books, 2014).

6. Hubert Joly and Caroline Lambert, *The Heart of Business: Leadership Principles for the Next Era of Capitalism* (Boston: Harvard Business Review Press, 2021).

7. Joly and Lambert, *Heart of Business*.

8. Rob Cross, Amy Edmondson, and Wendy Murphy, "A Noble Purpose Alone Won't Transform Your Company," *MIT Sloan Management Review*, December 10, 2019, https://sloanreview.mit.edu/article/a-noble-purpose -alone-wont-transform-your-company.

9. Association of National Advertisers (ANA), "B@B Companies Face 'Purpose Paradox,'" ANA press release, February 11, 2020, www.ana.net /content/show/id/pr-2020-purpose-paradox.

10. David Gelles, "Marc Benioff of Salesforce: 'Are We Not All Connected?'" *New York Times*, June 15, 2018, www.nytimes.com/2018/06/15 /business/marc-benioff-salesforce-corner-office.html.

11. Drew Neisser, "Singing the Praises of Small Business Saturday," *Fast Company*, November 12, 2012, www.fastcompany.com/3002870/singing -praises-small-business-Saturday.

12. Elena Schneider, "Honoring Small Business, Obamas Go Book Shopping," *New York Times*, November 29, 2014, www.nytimes.com/2014/11 /30/us/honoring-small-business-obamas-go-book-shopping.html.

13. Regina E. Herzlinger, "The Vitality Group: Paying for Self-Care," Case 9-310-071 (Boston: Harvard Business School, 2021).

14. Adrian Gore, "How Discovery Keeps Innovating," McKinsey & Company, June 2015, https://healthcare.mckinsey.com/how-discovery-keeps -innovating.

15. "Discovery Ltd.," Bloomberg, https://www.bloomberg.com/quote /DSY:SJ?sref=vyXbMhDm, accessed August 23, 2021.

16. Joly and Lambert, *Heart of Business*.

17. Andrew Ross Sorkin, "BlackRock's Message: Contribute to Society, or Risk Losing Our Support," *New York Times*, January 15, 2018, www .nytimes.com/2018/01/15/business/dealbook/blackrock-laurence-fink-letter .html.

18. Nathaniel Bullard, "How an Oil Company Becomes a Renewables Company," *Bloomberg Green*, May 6, 2021, www.bloomberg.com/news/articles/2021-05-06/the-climate-transition-how-an-oil-company-becomes-a-renewables-company.

19. See Equinor's "About Us" page at www.equinor.com/en/about-us.html, accessed July 22, 2021.

20. Breana Noble, "GM, Wabtec Partner for Zero-Emission Locomotives," *Detroit News*, June 15, 2021, www.detroitnews.com/story/business/autos/general-motors/2021/06/15/gm-wabtec-partner-zero-emission-locomotives-ultium-batteries-hydrotec-fuel-cells/7698018002.

Index

Acknowledgments

This book would not exist if it weren't for all the corporate change agents, entrepreneurs, and thought leaders who, at the start of the 2020 pandemic, joined together with a shared vision for a better world and helped launch the Go Forward to Work (GFTW) Institute. They include institute faculty members Peter Diamandis, Leo Tilman, Hubert Joly, Susan Sobbott, Mariya Filipova, Niko Canner, David Kidder, Mike Clementi, Najoh Tita-Reid, Taryn Marie Stejskal, Edward W. Sim, Michael Keithley, Rich Agostino, Angela Lane, Susan Quackenbush, Joselyn DiPetta, Todd Barrs, Ron Storn, Diana McKenzie, Sergey Gorbatov, Helen Russell, and Sandy Rezendes.

The research output from GFTW Institute, which forms the basis for each chapter, was generously cocreated and supported by partners like David Wilkie, Eric Lent, and Sydney Stroup at the World 50 organization; Tony Bingham and Ann Parker at ATD; Steven Raymond Beauchamp, Michael Haske, Jill Donohue, and Jen Deegan at Paylocity; Ranjit de Sousa, Michelle Anthony, Mary-Clare Race, and Frank Congiu at LHH; Mindy Grossman, Gail Tifford, Christy DeSantis, Mark Russo, and Tim Patno at WW; Michael Dell, Bobbie Maldonado, Susan Haas, Sara Downey, Jon Hyde, David Metta, and Trisha Pollock at Dell; Rob Locasio, Manlio Carrelli, Jon Borques, and Kate Twillmann at LivePerson; Carmine De Sibio, Mark Weinberger, Sarah Francis, Brittany Rooney, and Joe Dettman at EY; Frank Calderoni, Sara Baxter-Orr, Alice Hansen, and Adam Cooper at Anaplan; Marc Benioff, Jay Thayer, and Monica Youngblood at Salesforce; CeCe Morken and Whitney Bisplinghoff at Headspace; Sampath Sowmyanarayan, Jeff Dietel, Tami Erwin, Massimo Peselli, Stacy Cummings, Tony Delsignore, Denise Corbett, Amy Jefferson, Eric Spadafora, Jason Stevens, and Vikas Batra at Verizon; Dan Adika, Maor Ezer, and Shane Jackson at WalkMe; Adam Selipsky, Jackie Yeaney, Stephanie Richardson, and Rory Heath at Tableau; Rajiv Ramaswami, Qabil Shah, E. J. Bodnar, Pam Sanders, Cheryl Knight, Kathie Kuziel, and Ben Gibson at Nutanix; and Eric Mosley, Chris French, Patti Fletcher, Stacey Hinckley, Lauren Grady, Cara Bradley, Amy Rice, Jaime Castro, and Jill Kazanjian at Workhuman. We are deeply grateful for their vision and their commitment.

From Keith

Very special thanks goes to all my Friday-night family who kept me emotionally grounded throughout the pandemic and supported me through all the late nights and weekends of research and writing—Shadi, Josh, ChuChu, Seano, Michael, Blair, and Ben. And Austin, who went the crazy extra mile to bring agility and new technologies to my life and company. To my love, Kale, who inspired me to keep inspiring others and who, at every emotional dip, lifted me up. To my boys, Jacobo, Jack, and Tim, who are my constant and steady rudder. And, of course, thanks, Mom, for everything I am and am able to do for others.

I am grateful to contributing writer Paul Hill, who has pitched in for years every single time he was called, to my literary agent, Esmond Harmsworth at Aevitas Creative Management, for his wise strategic guidance and editorial comments, and to Noel Weyrich, who not only made everything happen but who has become a trusted friend! Thanks to my old friend and new cocreator Kian, who has been for years a great influence on my thinking about technology and disruption. And I can't thank Taryn Waters enough for her continued leadership and friendship.

From Kian

I thank my mother, Victoria Gohar, for her unconditional support. From a year of great disruption came opportunity, hope and love. And I thank my TLC writing family: Sam Horn, Peggy Cappy, Donna Steinhorn, Cherie Clark, Martin Rutte, and Elisabeth Misner.

From Keith, Kian, and Noel

Thanks to all of those who contributed in so many ways to the development of this manuscript on our expedited deadlines. For their generous direct contributions to these chapters, many thanks for the kind cooperation of Cathy Clegg, Pam Klyn, Telva McGruder, Mike Dennison, Eric Starkloff, Virgil Miller, Blake Voltz, Nicole Evans, Fabian Garcia, Dan Futter, Anup Sharma, Andy Sieg, David Frazee, Lindsay Keyser, Eddie Roger, Sarah Elk, Gary Foster, Jan Bruce, Bill Martin, Laura Chambers, Kristin Rand, Krystal Zell, Sera Lavelle, Sara Torres, Brenda Plechaty, Paula Wilbourne, Rick Ambrose, Jen Easterly, Jonathan Becher, David Reid, Eric Pulier, Colin Sprake, James DeJulio, Vijay Murugappan, Paul Hlivko, Rachel Sumekh, Dan Rifkin, Vinay Nadig, Aren Kaser, Jeff Miller, Dean Carter, Simon Mulcahy, Josh Silverman, Ivan Misner, and Chris Hyams. And for their help and advice as subject-matter experts, thanks to Nell Watson, Gayle Tzemach Lemmon, Matan Berkowitz, Kevin Noble, Andre Wegner, Avi Reichental, Dan Wellers, Clinton Bonner, Andy Hines, Matt Heller, and Marc Goodman.

Thanks also to all our peer reviewers who provided absolutely invaluable feedback: Angela Lane, Ozden Onder, Margaret Lazo, Amanda Hodges, Maarten Van Beek, James Sweeney, Nancy Lycan, Julieta Schuster, Ulrich Betz, Jeff Miller, and Thomas Birr.

To the entire team at Ferrazzi Greenlight, our deepest thanks for their tremendous efforts in keeping us all together and moving forward. Special thanks go to Jim Hannon, Keith's practical cofounder, and to Greg Seal, Keith's oldest and most trusted adviser and father figure. To Rob Whitfield and James Wakefield, who hold our foundation solid, and to Ronen Olshansky, Aaron Frankel, Alexa Geronimo, Amanda Bhardwaj, Kaitlyn Parent, John Galvin, and Patty Natili, who have breathed new life into our work and culture. And for their ceaseless creativity and hard work under difficult and unpredictable circumstances, thanks to Kimberly Stewart, Patrick Kealy, Eni Selfo, Ian Galvin, Deb Conrad, Austen Gardiner, Michele Mucio, and Nick Woloszyn. To Bruce Upbin and Karen Benezra, who began the GFTW journey and brought the heart, wisdom, and agility from the very start of this research.

Thanks to Adi Ignatius and Melinda Merino at Harvard Business Review Press, who saw the possibility of a new world of work emerging from months of crisis and uncertainty. And to the entire team at HBR Press, including Dan McGinn, executive editor at *Harvard Business Review*, and Sarah Moughty, executive editor at hbr.org, for their commitment to excellence all through the publishing process.

A final word of thanks goes to the many thousands of people who have participated in the work of the GFTW Institute and continue to co-elevate with us toward our shared purpose. The coming years will be years of profound uncertainty and unlimited opportunities. Our hope is that with your help, the GFTW Institute will be a beacon of insight and hope, always pressing us forward in this exciting new world of work.

About the Authors

KEITH FERRAZZI is the founder and chairman of Ferrazzi Greenlight, a management consulting and coaching company that works to transform many of the largest organizations and governments in the world. A graduate of Harvard Business School, Keith rose to become the youngest chief marketing officer of a *Fortune* 500 company during his career at Deloitte and later became CMO and head of sales at Starwood Hotels. He has contributed to *Harvard Business Review, Forbes, Fortune*, and the *Wall Street Journal* and is the *New York Times* number one bestselling author of *Who's Got Your Back, Never Eat Alone*, and *Leading Without Authority*. His mission is to transform teams to transform the world.

KIAN GOHAR inspires the world's leading organizations to harness innovation and moon shots to solve complex problems. A former executive director of the XPRIZE Foundation and Singularity University, Kian has coached the leadership teams of dozens of *Fortune* 500 companies. He is a sought-after public speaker on innovation and has been featured on CNBC, NPR, and Axios. He is a graduate of Northwestern University, the London School of Economics, and Harvard Business School.

NOEL WEYRICH has coauthored and edited more than twenty business leadership books and personal memoirs. He divides his time between Philadelphia and New York.

GO FORWARD TO WORK
REDEFINING THE FUTURE OF WORK, TODAY.

Go Forward to Work is an applied research institute that crowdsources best practices from thousands of C-suite executives across the globe in pursuit of revolutionizing the way we work.

LEARN MORE AND GET INVOLVED

Book a keynote

Access the latest insights on radical adaptability, hybrid collaboration, digital transformation, and employee well-being to move your business forward faster. Invite Keith Ferrazzi to speak to your teams or at your next event.

Request availability at **KeithFerrazzi.com/Speaking**

Join the research community

Build your network and elevate your personal brand, all while influencing the creation of best practices to help solve the most pressing challenges facing organizations today.

Apply at **GoForwardToWork.com/Community**

Partner with us

Generate new leads and engage your clients by helping us shape our research agenda. Your organization will be on the front lines of cutting-edge research and get a chance to be featured in major business publications.

Inquire at **GoForwardToWork.com/Partner**

FERRAZZI GREENLIGHT

TRANSFORMING TEAMS TO TRANSFORM THE WORLD

BRING RADICAL ADAPTABILITY TO LIFE WITH YOUR TEAM

Teams that embrace radical adaptability unleash unexpected growth and realize greater levels of success for their organizations.

We know this through our research efforts at **Go Forward to Work**, and it powers the work we do at Ferrazzi Greenlight.

Ferrazzi Greenlight exists to transform enterprises through executive team coaching.